MAGELLAN

and the First Voyage Around the World

MAGELLAN
and the First Voyage Around the World

BY NANCY SMILER LEVINSON

CLARION BOOKS
New York

Clarion Books
a Houghton Mifflin Company imprint
215 Park Avenue South, New York, NY 10003
Copyright © 2001 by Nancy Smiler Levinson
Maps copyright © 2001 by Kayley LeFaiver

The text was set in 14-point Spectrum.

www.houghtonmifflinbooks.com

Printed in the U.S.A.

Library of Congress Cataloging-in-Publication Data

Levinson, Nancy Smiler.
Magellan and the first voyage around the world / by Nancy Smiler Levinson.
p. cm.
Includes bibliographical references.
ISBN 0-395-98773-3
1. Magalhães, Fernão de, d. 1521—Journeys—Juvenile literature.
2. Voyages around the world—Juvenile literature. [1. Magellan, Ferdinand,
d. 1521 2. Explorers. 3. Voyages around the world.] I. Title.
G420.M2 L48 2001
910'.92—dc21
[B] 00-052350

CRW 10 9 8 7 6 5 4 3 2 1

For Irwin,
my dearest companion

CONTENTS

ACKNOWLEDGMENTS

My thanks are due to Diane C. Young, at the University of Minnesota Foundation, as well as to two University of Minnesota professors of history, Carla Rahv Phillips and Sara Chambers. Also helpful were Claudia A. Jew of the Mariners' Museum, Newport News, Virginia; Tim Joyner, historian and oceanographer; and Lucille Paradela-Fernandez, who shared her Philippine history.

I am grateful to my ever-patient husband and to my sons, Matthew and Daniel, my friend and colleague Joanne Rocklin, and my literary agent, Ruth Cohen, for their continued encouragement and steadfast support. I add thanks to Madeleine Comora, Caroline Arnold, Marjorie Cowley, Ann Whitford Paul, and Joan Hewett for their thoughtful comments and questions.

Finally, I wish to express special gratitude to my editor, Virginia Buckley, who has guided me with insight and integrity as I told this voyager's story.

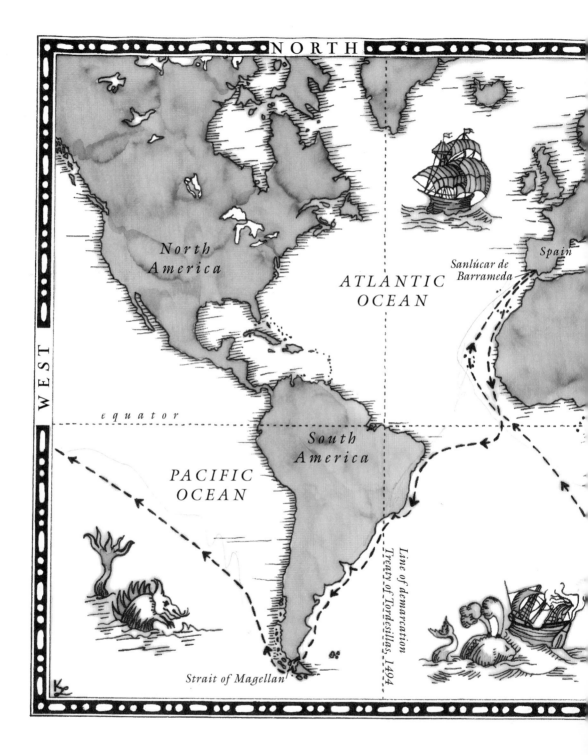

WEST

North
America

ATLANTIC
OCEAN

Sanlúcar de
Barrameda

Spain

equator

South
America

PACIFIC
OCEAN

Line of demarcation
Treaty of Tordesillas, 1494

Strait of Magellan

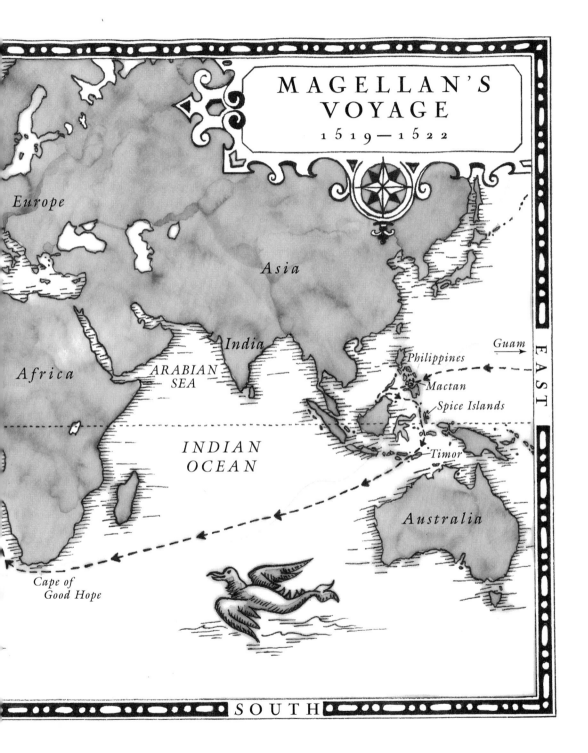

MAGELLAN'S VOYAGE
1519 — 1522

Europe

Asia

Africa

India

ARABIAN
SEA

INDIAN
OCEAN

Philippines

Guam

Mactan

Spice Islands

Timor

Australia

Cape of
Good Hope

EAST

SOUTH

Magellan, in a portrait by Antonio Menendez. MARINE MUSEUM, LISBON

CHAPTER ONE
Young Man of Portugal

Five centuries ago most people believed the world to be far smaller than it actually is. And while they understood that it's round—and not flat—they were convinced that it was not possible to circumnavigate the earth.

But ideas of the world's true size and the vastness of its ocean seas were about to change.

In 1513 a Spanish adventurer searching for gold led an expedition across the wild terrain of the Isthmus of Panama. This narrow stretch of land between two bodies of water in Central America could be explored only by foot. The adventurer, Vasco Núñez de Balboa, and his men pushed forward over rugged mountains and through tropical rain forests and dangerous, infested swamplands. Several of them died of disease or at the hands of natives along the way.

At last, after twenty-five days, the survivors reached the other side of the isthmus. On September 25, Balboa climbed atop a peak and gazed below. There he sighted an ocean. It was an ocean that no European had seen before. At once he realized that it was different from the known sea that separated Europe and the New World of the Americas—the Atlantic—which Christopher Columbus had sailed some twenty years earlier. Balboa named his find the Great South Sea. We know it as the Pacific Ocean.

Overcome with joy, Balboa raised his hands toward Heaven, thanked God and the saints for giving him the glory of making this "discovery," and, in the name of the Spanish crown, took possession "of all that sea and the countries bordering on it."

Balboa never set sail on that ocean. He died a few years later. But someone would soon attempt to cross it, even though no one had any notion of its expanse or how long a crossing might take or how dangerous it might be.

In the early 1500s, Europe was in the midst of an important age of exploration. Seafaring nations were eager to conquer new lands and seas, gain riches, and expand their empires. Their rulers encouraged exploring and financed one expedition after another.

It was only six years after Balboa's sighting that a daring and determined mariner set sail across that unknown ocean. His voyage would become the most remarkable and perilous one in seafaring history. It would bring final proof that the world was round, that its circumference was great indeed, and that the earth was circumnavigable. We know this explorer as Ferdinand Magellan.

He was born Fernão de Magalhães in Portugal, in 1480 or possibly a few years earlier. Records of his precise birthdate and the place of his birth no longer exist, but documents suggest that he lived first in Portugal's rugged, mountainous northwest district of Nobrega and later in the commercial seaport center of Porto.

His mother was Alda de Mesquita, and his father was Ruy de Magalhães. His father was descended from a family of minor nobility and had been awarded an honorary position guarding a port town near Porto. Ferdinand had a sister, Isabel; his older brother, Diogo, took the last name of their paternal grandmother, de Sousa, so that he could later inherit part of that family's estate.

In Nobrega the family lived in a two-story farmhouse. They occupied the upper floor, while the lower floor was used as a stable for cattle, sheep, and goats. Like their neighbors, they raised wheat, rye, and milho, a variety of maize special to the region that was ground into cornmeal. Nearby vineyards provided grapes, which children often helped their parents make into wine.

The Magalhães family was Catholic and worshiped regularly at a large stone cathedral. On holidays children marched in choral procession through the narrow, winding streets.

Most boys attended school at church or were taught by traveling tutors. At first, Ferdinand and Diogo studied the catechism, Latin, and arithmetic at a nearby monastery school. Later, since their father claimed minor aristocracy, they were able to enter into service at the Portuguese court as pages. There they performed the duties of ushering, running errands, and keeping order in the royal chambers. Ferdinand was probably between twelve and fourteen when he served at Queen Leonora's court in Lisbon.

The harbor at Lisbon, from a painting by Theodor de Bry. NORTH WIND PICTURE ARCHIVES

As pages, the boys were entitled to an advanced education. They were schooled in reading, writing, arithmetic, religion, and venery—hunting with hawk and hound. They were instructed in music, dancing, horsemanship, and fencing, too. Tutors also taught them a subject that was especially important to Portugal: nautical studies, which included astronomy and navigation. It's likely that studying these lessons, as well as hearing stories of sailing to fascinating, far-away places, made the country boy Ferdinand yearn to go to sea.

Lisbon was the capital of Portugal and a center of seafaring activity. For a long time Portugal had encouraged the study of the science of navigation. The man who had led the way half a century earlier was

Prince Henrique, known as Henry the Navigator. At Sagres on Cape Vincent he had established a school where he gathered from all over the world mariners, mapmakers, and cosmographers—men who studied the structure and physical features of the universe.

Under Prince Henry's guidance, the men built ships increasingly

Prince Henry the Navigator. NATIONAL LIBRARY, PARIS

better suited to long voyages and coastal exploring. They also sailed to the Cape Verde Islands and later ventured farther and farther south along the eastern coast of Africa, establishing trade in ivory and gold, as well as the earliest institution of the African slave trade by sea.

As Ferdinand was growing up, he was well aware of the fervor to explore and to gain ever-greater wealth. He knew that Portugal had the lead over its strongest rival, Spain. But Spain's sea power was increasing. Finally, Spain became such a strong and threatening competitor that Portugal's king, John (João) II, began keeping news of all Portuguese discoveries secret.

The most closely guarded discovery had occurred in 1488. King John had sent a mariner, Bartolomeu Dias, along the African Gold Coast to chart the distance from Portugal as far south as possible toward the Indian Ocean. But a hurricane blew Dias's ship so far off course that he ended up actually rounding Africa's tip, which he named the Cape of Storms. Soon Dias realized that he had reached the Indian Ocean. He was astonished at this turn of events. He had found a new sea route. That was great news to King John, who vowed to send out more and more expeditions. These journeys were filled with hardships and danger, however, and so to encourage seamen to sign on, King John changed the name of the Cape of Storms to the Cape of Good Hope.

Meanwhile, Spain financed the four voyages of Christopher Columbus as he searched for a western route to the fabulous East Indies, now called Asia. He never reached the East Indies, but he

Christopher Columbus. CIVIC NAVAL MUSEUM OF GENOA AT PEGLI

claimed for Spain all the islands he found along the way. King John was greatly upset when he learned of this, insisting that Columbus had sailed wrongfully through Portuguese territorial waters.

In order to solve the problem of rivalry in territorial expansion, in 1493 Pope Alexander VI issued a papal bull. This was a formal treaty in which he decreed a division of claims "by the authority of almighty God." The Pope imagined a line north to south through the Atlantic Ocean, about 100 leagues west of the Cape Verde Islands. (A league is 2.82 nautical miles. A nautical mile is slightly longer than a mile as we know it.)

This line of demarcation, which was an estimation, went through the North and South Poles and circled the other half of the globe. Spain would claim all discoveries to the west of the line in the Atlantic, while Portugal would take those to the east.

A year later the line was refixed at 370 leagues, or about 1,043 nautical miles, west of the Azores and Cape Verde Islands, giving Portugal part of what is now Brazil. The new line of demarcation was declared in the Treaty of Tordesillas.

In reality, however, it was impossible to divide or possess distant territories of the globe. No one really knew where the imaginary line lay on the other side of the world, because no one then knew the actual size of the world or what existed there.

The desire for conquest was certainly an important reason to explore. But the real prize was the Spice Islands, also known as the Moluccas. These islands were in the central East Indies, or what is now Indonesia, and lay between what is now Sulawesi (Celebes) and

New Guinea. Treasures considered more valuable than gold and gems, silks and furs, or the finest of horses were to be found there. The treasures were spices culled from plants—cloves, cinnamon, and nutmeg, which flavored food and were used to mask tainted meats.

One spice was the most highly profitable of all: pepper. Europeans and Muslims from the East who sought pepper because it was especially long-lasting and easy to trade called it black gold.

When Ferdinand Magellan lived as a page at court, he listened eagerly to stories of sea travel and treasure hunts for spices. He heard tales of how Dias was blown to the Indian Ocean and how another seaman, Pedro de Covilhão, had been sent in disguise as an Arab merchant to gather information about trade routes to India. And he heard all kinds of exotic tales about Columbus's first voyage of 1492–93. It's easy to imagine how young Magellan began to dream of his own seafaring adventures.

Meanwhile, King John was expanding Portuguese trading and shipping at ports on Africa's east coast and along the west coast of India. Arab merchants there troubled him, however. Not only were they interfering in his business, but King John, a Christian, opposed them because they were Muslims, who didn't worship Christ.

Then, in 1495, King John suddenly died. It was rumored that his wife, Queen Leonora, had poisoned him so that her brother Manuel (Manoel) could ascend the throne. King John and Queen Leonora had had a son, but he had died in 1491 under mysterious circumstances, so there was no direct heir. Moreover, the families of the king and queen had been enemies, and Leonora wished to promote her own family at court.

Manuel I was crowned king of Portugal. He was called Manuel the Fortunate because he inherited vast wealth from Portuguese commerce. Rich as he was, he dreamed of expanding the Portuguese Empire even further.

When Manuel came to power, Ferdinand and the other pages in Leonora's court were removed to the king's court and placed at King Manuel's disposal. The new ruler quickly revealed himself to be a harsh and insensitive man. Worse, for Ferdinand, he showed an especially strong dislike of him, even though the boy took care to act respectfully and to perform his duties well. Ferdinand could never understand the reason for Manuel's unkind treatment. One historian has suggested that the cause was family rivalry. Another thinks that Ferdinand and Diogo, country boys, were regarded as lowly at court.

However, when Ferdinand's duties as page ended, he was allowed to remain in royal service instead of being dismissed altogether. He was sent to Mina House, an official agency that supervised exploration and merchant sailing. He was assigned to the job of clerk, where day by day he was exposed to mapmaking and globe making, shipbuilding, and discussions on theories of sailing and trade. He learned about rigging, repairing, arming, and loading ships. He also learned how to prepare large quantities of foodstuffs, such as biscuits, and how to seal wine in casks for storage on long journeys. He worked hard, yearning to set sail himself but fearing that he would never have the chance to go to sea.

Meanwhile, in 1497, King Manuel sent Vasco da Gama on an exploring expedition. Da Gama rounded the Cape of Good Hope at the tip of Africa and was the first to successfully reach India by sea and open a new trade route. He returned in 1499 with spices, gems, and information about sailing, merchandising, and naval wars. The king was so pleased that he secretly ordered more expeditions, many of which involved spying on Spain's part of the world. In one, the mariner Pedro Álvares Cabral, sailing too far off the African coast, accidentally reached Brazil and took possession of it for Portugal.

After sending thousands of men to sea in the eight years since da Gama's expedition, Portugal was drained of experienced sailors. Still, Mina House grew and was renamed India House, indicating that it would concentrate all its efforts on making gains in that region. Magellan, a young man who kept his thoughts to himself, continued to work diligently and loyally as a clerk in the king's service, waiting for his time to come.

King Manuel I. Marine Museum, Lisbon

CHAPTER TWO

War Campaigns at Sea

During the years that Magellan worked at India House, the wealthy King Manuel dreamed of acquiring even greater wealth. He already controlled many ports of trade in Africa and India. But these weren't enough for him.

He decided that Portugal must master the Indian Ocean and take control of all ports of trade. He realized this would not be easy, so he worked out an ambitious plan. It would require a great naval war campaign—he would send a fleet of twenty-two heavily armed ships under the command of a viceroy, Francisco de Almeida.

As soon as Magellan learned of the plan, he offered his service at sea. King Manuel still scorned Magellan, but with a shortage of seamen, he badly needed crew. He had little choice but to give his young, loyal subject permission to sign on.

At last, Magellan would be able to fulfill his seafaring ambition.

Coast at Cochin and Cannanore. The next part of the plan called for taking the ports at Calicut, Goa, and Cambay. However, the Portuguese were facing more and more trouble in India. Egyptian forces had strengthened Arab and Hindu naval power against them. Sea battles were becoming increasingly bloody.

Badly needing reinforcement, Almeida dispatched an order to Magellan's small fleet to sail to India at once. When the support arrived, the commander put his son in charge of a flotilla. But in a surprise Egyptian attack Almeida's son was slaughtered, along with one hundred men. Magellan and Pereira were spared the attack because they had gone ashore to repair their caravel.

Almeida was so enraged at his son's death and the destruction of his squadron that he wasted no time in taking revenge. He found the enemy ships near the city of Dabul (now Dapoli) and bombarded them in a massive assault. Then, in an excessively cruel massacre, he destroyed the city and killed all its citizens. When he was finished there, he attacked the port of Diu. This time Magellan and Pereira did not escape battle. At Diu, Pereira was killed and Magellan was badly wounded. He was taken to a Portuguese hospital in Cochin, where he spent four months recovering. For his service in battle, he received partial pay of twenty sacks of wheat, as is shown by his signature on a receipt.

Despite the losses and the bloodshed, Portugal was gaining control of the Indian Ocean. In March 1509, four years after the campaign began, King Manuel decided the time was right for a change in command, and he replaced Almeida with another viceroy,

Malabar Coast, India. Courtesy of Madeleine Comora

Affonso de Albuquerque. Albuquerque set new sights on conquering Malacca, a settlement near Malaya and the gateway to the Moluccas—the highly prized Spice Islands. Magellan and his friend Serrão joined the campaign, but while they were anchored off Malacca, they were ambushed and lost thirty men. In the midst of the attack, Magellan realized that Serrão had gone ashore and was in danger of being captured. Magellan jumped into a skiff, rowed ashore, and courageously rescued his friend and several other men.

Not long afterward, during a battle with a Chinese junk—a heavy cargo ship—Magellan saved Serrão's life again. Albuquerque heard about the strong, fearless Magellan and rewarded him with a caravel of his own and the rank of captain. After years of service, Magellan had been recognized at last.

Magellan joined a raid on Calicut, but he suffered another wound, this time in the leg. By now Magellan had been in battles for five years. He had won honor and rank. He had collected a supply of pepper, which would bring a good price in Portugal. But he was injured and weary, and he saw a dim future for himself if he remained. He heard of a caravel about to sail for Portugal, and he asked for and was granted permission to go home.

Unfortunately, because of a pilot's error, the ship ran aground. During the rescue of the sailors, Magellan went to the aid of the

Pepper plant. COURTESY OF MADELEINE COMORA

lower-ranked men, which was not commonly done by ships' officers. This generous act earned him a good reputation as a fair and loyal officer.

All the pepper aboard the ship was ruined, however. Magellan despaired. How could he return home empty-handed and with no prospect of future work? He had little choice but to return to the king's service.

This time Magellan was assigned to join an attack on the city of Goa. After suffering heavy losses, the men had to retreat. On a second attempt, they captured the city, brutally killing eight thousand Muslim men, women, and children. Goa subsequently became the center of Portuguese trade power and remained a Portuguese colony until 1961. It is still the only part of India with a large Christian population.

Once more Albuquerque turned his attention to Malacca. This was a harbor of international trade, where Chinese junks and Arab dhows came and went. Spices, gems, porcelain, ivory, cashmere, sake (a Japanese alcoholic drink), and slaves were bought and sold. The scene dazzled the eye, exotic scents filled the air, and many languages were heard at every turn.

Albuquerque sent nineteen warships to fight the sultan of Malacca and his large army. Following six weeks of bloody battles, the Portuguese triumphed in securing the key of this gateway to riches. Albuquerque had completed his mission of winning naval supremacy on the Indian Ocean.

It is likely that Magellan remained in Malacca after its conquest

A ship of Albuquerque's fleet. NORTH WIND PICTURE ARCHIVES

in 1511, gathering information on navigation and the geography of the region. Even though there are no records showing Magellan's precise whereabouts during that time, one event is certain: he acquired a young slave. His name was Enrique, and he was fourteen years old. He became a loyal servant and companion to Magellan throughout the explorer's life.

Scholars have speculated that during this period Magellan sailed on secret voyages that may have brought him near the Spice Islands. Caravels did secretly explore waters in the region. Fellow seaman Francisco Serrão commanded one such voyage. In fact, when Serrão's caravel was destroyed in a monsoon storm, native rescuers guided him to the Spice Island of Ternate. And there on that island of paradise Serrão stayed, never to return to Portugal again.

Magellan knew of Serrão's whereabouts because he received letters from him, delivered by Chinese junks. Serrão wrote, urging Magellan to come and live in royal splendor, and Magellan imagined joining his friend there someday, once he had made his fortune.

In 1513, after eight years away from home, Magellan, accompanied by Enrique, finally returned to Portugal. He had endured siege and shipwreck, weariness and injury. But he had also gained respect and rank. Was it not time for the tide to turn?

In Portugal, however, nothing went well for him. A merchant with whom he had made a business deal, and who owed him money, had died. At court, Magellan learned that he was still regarded as a lowly man in royal service. Little had changed. Magellan was truly discouraged. Yet he was iron willed and refused to see himself as defeated.

What else could he do but join one last expedition? King Manuel, despite the great wealth gained after his brutal campaign to gain control of the Indian Ocean, grew greedier and more despotic. He already controlled trade in the North African port capital city of Morocco, but people there were rebelling, and he wanted them punished. Magellan and his brother, who also joined the expedition, were assigned to a cavalry unit. The city surrendered early, but Magellan suffered a lance wound to his knee, so deep he would never again walk without a limp.

Back home in the royal court of Portugal, Magellan once more found himself completely ignored by King Manuel. Month after month Magellan watched other men gain high positions and salaries through intrigue and patronage, and not based on their merits. The injustice struck him deeply.

During this time rumors began to spread throughout the court: Spain was preparing an expedition to explore the western coast of Central America. Magellan's mind began to spin with visions of sailing westward to the Spice Islands. He had acquired a mariner's knowledge of the region. He possessed a good collection of charts and maps. He was convinced that such an expedition was his destiny. Surely, now the king would recognize and praise him.

But the king refused Magellan a private audience. He allowed Magellan to approach only on the day he received commoners. How humiliating for Magellan! Without complaining, he steeled himself and stood patiently in line. When it was his turn to bow before the king and make his request, Manuel turned him down. Disgraced, yet still determined, Magellan fell to his knees and begged to learn how he might serve his majesty.

The king answered that he had no further interest in Magellan. Finally, Magellan asked permission to serve another country. Glad to be rid of the man he disliked so much, King Manuel waved Magellan away.

CHAPTER THREE
The Great Enterprise

erdinand Magellan was now an outcast in his own land. What country would accept him and finance his westward voyage? He considered Italy, but its once great seapower was declining. England, Holland, and France were more interested in exploring the world's northern regions. The only country left was Portugal's rival, Spain.

Meanwhile, Magellan settled in Porto, where he had spent part of his youth. His sister lived there, and his brother had returned there after the war campaigns. Porto was a lively seaport center where pilots and cosmographers gathered from many nations to exchange ideas and further their knowledge. With nothing but the vision of the enterprise on his mind, Magellan threw himself into the study of maps, nautical charts, and the latest methods of navigation.

The science of navigation had been steadily advancing since Columbus's voyages. Columbus had navigated by dead reckoning, plotting his course and position by direction, time, and speed; he had had to determine speed as best he could by watching a "fixed" point, an object like a cloud formation or a piece of floating seaweed. He had also used a compass, although it wasn't scientifically accurate, since little was known about the pull exerted on the compass by the earth's magnetic field.

Mariners were learning more precise ways to determine latitude—the distance measured in degrees above and below the equator. Longitude—a system of north to south imaginary lines to indicate east or west position on the earth—was impossible to measure accurately until the invention of the marine chronometer by Englishman John Harrison in the eighteenth century. Before then, mariners had been limited to making rough estimations. Pilots used quadrants or astrolabes, devices that measured angles formed by celestial bodies over the horizon, to help fix the position of a ship in open seas. With these instruments they calculated latitude by measuring the altitude of the sun from the horizon or the altitude of the Pole Star (North Star), which remains constant.

At the same time that Magellan was immersing himself in his studies, another Portuguese outcast also took up residence in Porto. He was Ruy Faleiro, a university-educated mathematician who was fascinated with astronomy and celestial navigation—sailing by observing celestial bodies. While living at court in Portugal, he had hoped to win an appointment as royal astronomer, but

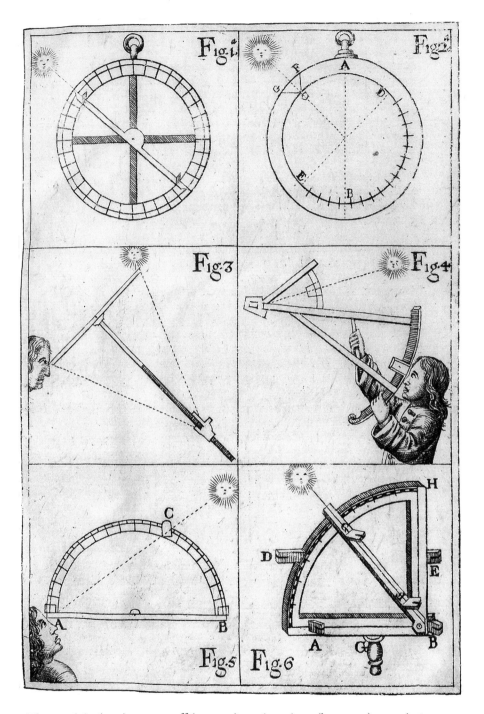

The astrolabe (top), cross-staff (center), and quadrant (bottom) were devices to measure the angles formed by certain stars over the horizon. The measurements helped to fix the position of the ship on the vast expanse of the ocean.

instead he, too, had been snubbed by King Manuel. Faleiro was considered a highly intelligent man; sometimes he behaved oddly and was given to wild outbursts of temper, and that may have been a principal reason for his dismissal.

Magellan and Faleiro met soon after the mathematician's arrival. Despite the contrast between the calm and stoic Magellan and the temperamental Faleiro, they forged a relationship founded on common interests.

By this time Magellan was convinced beyond any doubt that he could reach the Spice Islands by following a *western* route, and according to the line of demarcation, any such islands belonged to Spain. Magellan also firmly believed that there was a seaway passage

---

ASTROLABE AND QUADRANT

The *astrolabe* was a heavy disk with degrees marked around its edges and a rotating arm with small holes at either end. The pilot held out the disk while another man moved the arm until a sunbeam shone through the hole at one end and fell on the hole at the other. The arm indicated the sun's altitude by the disk's marked degrees. On a rolling sea or in a storm, however, neither instrument was usable.

A *quadrant* was a quarter circle of wood or brass measuring zero to ninety degrees. There were tiny sight holes on each end of its straight edges. The pilot lined up the sights on the Pole Star, while an affixed plumb line hung down over the curved area. The specific point of intersection indicated the height of the star in latitude degrees.

---

in South America to get from the Atlantic Ocean to the ocean beyond.

That ocean was the Great South Sea, which had been sighted by Balboa only three years earlier, in 1513. But so far no European had been able to reach the Great South Sea by ship.

How did Magellan become so sure that a sea passage existed? While he was still living in Portugal, he had heard stories about some of King Manuel's secretly ordered voyages. On one such voyage two explorers had sailed around the bulge of Brazil and reported finding a passage entrance at latitude 35°, a cape at the mouth of a river now called Río de la Plata. They didn't enter it, however, for fear of being caught trespassing in Spanish territory. Then, on another voyage, an explorer ventured a short distance into what he believed to be the passage, but he was killed by natives of the region.

It was not long after Magellan and Faleiro met that they began making plans to lead a westward expedition to the Spice Islands. Together they would go to Spain and present details of their enterprise to the Spanish king. Magellan was so full of hope that he was certain the king would grant them support. He expressed his optimistic feelings in letters to Francisco Serrão on the Spice Island of Ternate. One letter is preserved: "God willing, I will soon be seeing you, whether by way of Portugal or Castile [Spain], for that is the way my affairs have been leading. You must wait for me there, because we already know that it will be some time before we can expect things to get better for us."

Magellan and Faleiro's plans were completed in 1517, and they

SPAIN AND PORTUGAL

NORTH

FRANCE

WEST

EAST

Porto

Valladolid

SPAIN

PORTUGAL

Lisbon

Guadalquivir R.

Seville
Sanlúcar de
Barrameda

Cádiz

Mediterranean Sea

Atlantic
Ocean

AFRICA

SOUTH

set a departure time for Spain. Magellan would leave in October. Faleiro was to follow several weeks later. Meanwhile, they swore secrecy: They would not speak of their enterprise until they joined up again.

Magellan renounced his Portuguese citizenship. He bade his brother and sister farewell. It was a painful time, and he wondered whether he would ever see his family or the country of his birth again.

Ferdinand Magellan arrived in Seville, Spain, on October 20, 1517. Enrique, his loyal servant, and a boy named Cristovão Rebêlo accompanied him. Magellan called Rebêlo his page, but historians suggest that the boy probably was Magellan's illegitimate son. It was not unusual for men at court or in the church to have illegitimate sons, whom they called nephew or page.

Magellan was now living as an expatriate in Spain. He was not the only expatriate there, because many pilots and businessmen had also renounced their Portuguese citizenship and taken up residency in that country. The businessmen were especially interested in making connections with the royal court and with European bankers willing to finance or invest in sailing expeditions, secret or otherwise. With such associations, they could make handsome profits.

A shrewd international banking family, the Fuggers, and their partner and agent, Cristóbal de Haro, were the most influential. Like King Manuel, Haro had also financed secret voyages while living in Portugal, creating a clash between the two and resulting in Manuel's driving Haro out of Portugal.

Another man of authority was the expatriate Diogo Barbosa. He was a clever businessman who had made a fortune in the spice trade and had gained influence as an adviser at the Spanish court. Since he had a son who knew Magellan from their years together in the Indian Ocean campaign, Barbosa arranged a meeting with Magellan as soon as the newcomer arrived in Spain.

Barbosa not only welcomed Magellan into his large, splendid home; within months he had even arranged a wedding between Magellan and his daughter, Beatriz. This turned out to be advantageous for Magellan, because his host and new father-in-law would introduce him to people in the best positions to help him win support for his enterprise.

Two of the most noted Spanish men whom Magellan met were Juan de Aranda and Bishop Juan Rodríguez de Fonseca. Aranda was manager of the Casa de Contratación de las Indias, an agency that oversaw maritime matters and preparations for exploring expeditions, as well as the agency's adviser to the Spanish court. When Aranda heard rumors of Magellan's plan, he saw a good business opportunity for himself.

Bishop Rodríguez de Fonseca was a clergyman at court. He was sly and scheming, and he held strong political and business ambitions. He had an illegitimate son, Juan de Cartagena, whom he called nephew and who would play a major role later in Magellan's life. The bishop had gained his power at court during the earlier rule of King Ferdinand and Queen Isabella. They were the sovereigns who had financed Columbus's voyages. After their deaths, their grandson, sixteen-year-old Charles (Carlos) I, was named successor to the throne.

As soon as Bishop Fonseca learned about Magellan's plan, he sealed a secret partnership with Haro, who could hardly wait to take revenge on King Manuel for driving him out of Portugal. Haro promised that if the bishop could convince the royal court to sponsor Magellan's voyage, Haro would offer substantial financing for it. Now it was up to the bishop to persuade the new young king to grant Magellan an audience. If the king refused, then there would be no enterprise at all.

When Charles I was proclaimed king in 1516, he was living in Flanders (in northern Europe), where he had been cared for by an aunt. But his advisers did not prepare him to travel to Spain until the following year. Accompanied by a cortege of Flemish courtiers, he arrived at the royal court in Valladolid in November 1517, a month after Magellan had set foot in Seville.

Charles was seventeen years old. He spoke no Spanish. He was small and rather homely, but he was considered dignified. Having had no playmates as a child, he had spent his time alone and had developed a keen interest in animals, mechanical devices, and detailed maps. Because the king was so young and just beginning to study the Spanish language, Bishop Fonseca took advantage of the situation and seized authority at court. He even helped himself to large sums from the royal treasury.

A month after Charles had arrived in Spain, Magellan's partner,

King Charles I. ALINARI ARCHIVES, FLORENCE

Ruy Faleiro, left Portugal. When Faleiro found out that people everywhere knew about their plan, he became enraged that their sworn pact had been meaningless, and threatened to end the partnership.

Meanwhile, arrangements were made for both men to appear before King Charles. Juan de Aranda organized their journey on horseback from Seville to the court in Valladolid in early 1518. Magellan, Faleiro, and Enrique rode with a cavalcade to protect them against thieves and highway robbers. Aranda, always thinking of rewards for himself, had good reason to make sure the journey was safeguarded. As an exchange for his efforts, he bargained with Magellan to receive a portion of the profits. In a contract they signed, Magellan agreed to give Aranda one eighth of the amount the partners stood to earn. Magellan signed his name Hernando de Magallanes. This contract is believed to be the first time that the Portuguese expatriate signed his name using Spanish spelling.

The cavalcade arrived at Valladolid on February 16. It was unusual for the court to receive visitors without lengthy delays, so it was surprising that the partners were admitted quickly and with little trouble. First they met with Charles's ministers, and only a few days later they were welcomed by King Charles himself.

The confident Magellan made a calm, convincing presentation, stating each point precisely and purposefully. The first and most important goal was to reach the Spice Islands. The aim was to sail westward rather than take the familiar eastern route. That would prove that the islands were in Spanish territorial waters. Contrary to myth, Magellan never intended to sail with the grand purpose of circumnavigating the globe.

Once Magellan saw that he had the king's attention, he explained that Spain stood to gain great profits from the spice trade. And what high pride the Spanish nation would also win! Next, Magellan showed Francisco Serrão's letters from the island of Ternate and introduced Enrique, who came from the region and spoke the Malayan language.

Then, Magellan and Faleiro displayed a hand-painted leather globe. One court observer, Bishop Bartolomé de Las Casas, described it as "a globe in which the whole world was depicted."

Referring to it as *el paso*, the globe indicated an entrance to a fabled seaway passage in South America that Magellan believed ran between two land masses. We call such a passage a strait. But Magellan did not point out the entrance to the king. He was intent on keeping the information to himself.

Finally, Magellan assured the king that he, Ferdinand Magellan, was a gentleman of noble ancestry, as well as a man of experience at sea.

Bishop Las Casas later wrote: "Magellan must have been a man of courage, valiant in both his thoughts and in undertaking great things, although he was not of imposing presence, since he was small in stature and did not appear to be much."

The young king had been listening keenly and with an open mind. He found Magellan's idea and aim promising. He thought that the painted globe and the scientific discussion were especially

Letter of October 24, 1518, written by Magellan to King Charles, proposing taxation to help finance the expedition to the Spice Islands. GENERAL ARCHIVE OF THE INDIES, SEVILLE

interesting. And he saw Magellan as an impressive, persuasive, and personally likable man.

All along, Magellan had believed that he would win the court's support, although he had thought it would take a long time—perhaps even months. But King Charles surprised him. He approved the enterprise only a few weeks after Magellan presented it. The king then made an even more startling announcement: He, and he alone, would finance the voyage.

The men surrounding Magellan were shocked and angry at this. If they weren't allowed to invest, how could they reap rewards for themselves? Bishop Fonseca was especially furious at his loss of power and jealous of the attention the king paid Magellan. No one, though, was more astonished by the decision than Magellan himself.

A contract was signed, granting Magellan and Faleiro the title of governor of any islands they discovered, as well as possession of two islands once they had discovered six. After expenses they were to receive five percent of revenues from their discovered lands and a twenty-percent share of profits from the spice cargo of their first voyage. Charles wrote and signed: "You have my royal words that I protect you, as I hereby give the signature of my name. Valladolid, on the 22nd of March, 1518. I the King."

At last Magellan felt blessed with fortune. But the businessmen and royal advisers became as bitter and jealous as the bishop. They were not about to forget the enterprise and their lost chances at making a profit. Indeed, their interference and evil scheming behind Magellan's back would beset him with ever-growing troubles.

CHAPTER FOUR
fitting Out the fleet

Preparation of Magellan's fleet began at once. Upon royal order, Juan de Aranda traveled to Cádiz, where he purchased five ships built of oak and arranged to have them brought upriver to Seville to be fitted out. They were not new, though, because the expense of building such a squadron would have been prohibitive. Instead, they were sea worn and in need of extensive repair.

The names of the ships were the *Trinidad*, Magellan's flagship, *San Antonio*, *Concepción*, *Victoria*, and *Santiago*.

Four were carracks, or *naos*, large cargo-carrying merchant ships with big, square sails, best fit for long ocean voyages. The *Santiago* was a caravel, with lateen, or triangular, sails. It was smaller, lighter, and swifter—well suited to coastal exploring in shallow waters. All of them had three masts—foremast, mainmast, and mizzenmast. And each carried a batelle, a two-masted longboat that was towed, as well as a few skiffs—small oared boats that were stowed on deck. These boats were especially important for approaching unknown coasts and for rowing ashore.

The size of a ship was stated as its cargo capacity—an ancient method that used the capacity of wine casks, or barrels, as a stan-

Sixteenth-century shipbuilding on the Central American coast.
SEAVER CENTER FOR WESTERN HISTORY RESEARCH, NATURAL HISTORY MUSEUM OF LOS ANGELES COUNTY

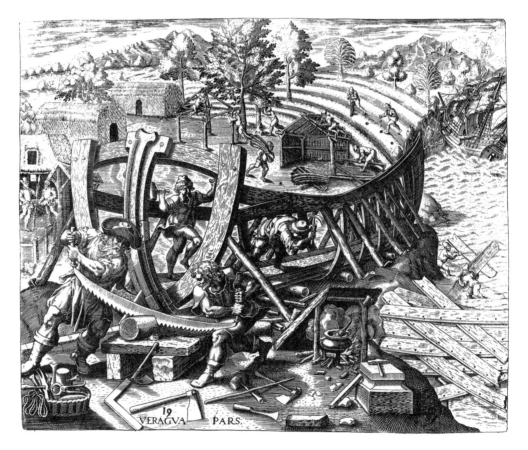

dard of measurement. The space occupied by two casks was called a *tonelada* and represented about 975 quarts. In Magellan's time an average ship measured 100 *toneladas* in capacity and was about 85 feet in length—small in comparison to ships that sail the seas today.

The estimated *tonelada* measurement of the fleet's largest ship, the *San Antonio*, was 120. That of the caravel, the *Santiago*, was 75.

From the start, Magellan excitedly threw himself into helping fit out the fleet. He worked alongside the laborers day and night, making repairs, purchasing supplies and stores, and overseeing even the smallest details, such as flag and banner design. This work went on throughout most of 1518 and into the following summer.

Magellan also paid close attention to the recruitment of his crew, not an easy task. Since there were so many expeditions for both exploring and trading, there was a shortage of able seamen. When recruiters did find some, most of them refused to join the expedition because they would have been required to sign on for a full two years, which was a long time to spend at sea. Not only that, they weren't even given the destination. Magellan insisted on keeping his plans to himself, fearing that other explorers might find out about them and get to the Spice Islands first.

Recruiting agents were sent out to several countries until they finally managed to assemble enough men to make up five crews. While the majority of the seamen were Spanish and Portuguese, there were also French, Flemish, Italian, German, Greek, Irish, Moorish, African, Asian, and English crew members. Personnel records are imprecise. The most accepted total number is 270.

Unfortunately, angry arguments about crew selection arose in Seville at the start. Bishop Fonseca and Haro complained to the court that Magellan was taking on too many Portuguese. They insisted that the number be restricted, and they won their argument. The matter of who was most fit to command each ship caused further wrangling. Three Spanish captains were eventually approved, but the scheming bishop turned them all against Magellan, calling him a foreigner who couldn't be trusted. Those three captains would become Magellan's worst enemies at sea.

Later, when Bishop Fonseca and Haro found out that Magellan and Faleiro had promised a profit percentage to Juan de Aranda of the Casa de Contratación, they vengefully succeeded in getting Aranda demoted from his managerial position. Finally, the bishop and Haro saw to it that their own family members were assigned high rank in the fleet. Bishop Fonseca's son, Juan de Cartagena, was named captain of the *San Antonio* as well as fleet inspector general to guard against possible betrayal by foreign officers.

Spaniards Gaspar de Quesada and Luis de Mendoza were selected captains of the *Concepcíon* and the *Victoria*. The two Portuguese captains were Magellan on the *Trinidad* and João Serrão on the *Santiago*.

Other officers' positions, such as ships' masters and pilots, were filled, and craftsmen, priests, barber-surgeons, laborers, and artillerymen were divided among the fleet. Personal servants accompanied a few of the officers. One of them was Enrique, who was highly valued as an interpreter since he spoke the Malayan language, and Magellan made sure that he was paid a higher wage than servants of some of

Model of the Victoria. THE MARINERS' MUSEUM, NEWPORT NEWS, VIRGINIA

This document declares: "Roll of the people going in the ships bound to the Indies and the discovery of the Spice Islands, of which Fernando de Magallanes was Captain General." GENERAL ARCHIVES OF THE INDIES, SEVILLE

the officers. Magellan also watched over another boy on the *Trinidad*—Cristovão Rebêlo.

Then, shortly before departure, a young Italian adventurer, about twenty-eight years old, arrived in Seville. He was not an able seaman. He was born of a noble family in Vicenza and had hardly any sailing experience. His name was Antonio Pigafetta.

While traveling in Spain, Pigafetta had become acquainted with the Vatican ambassador to the Spanish court. When the ambassador told him about the expedition, Pigafetta's imagination was sparked, and he asked permission to join as an observer. He intended, as he wrote later, "to experience the great and terrible things of the Ocean Sea" and perhaps "win a famous name with posterity."

The ambassador liked the idea of having an observer take note of the line of demarcation for the pope, so he approved Pigafetta's request at once. Magellan and the Casa de Contratación accepted the young man as a "supernumerary," the title Magellan had held when he first went to sea in the Indian Ocean campaign.

Little else is known of Pigafetta's life. But as observer and journal keeper, he would become one of the most valuable men both on the voyage and for later historians.

Magellan knew the voyage would be long, requiring vast amounts of stores and supplies, navigational equipment, and artillery and firearms. So he went to great lengths to be sure that all his anticipated needs would be met by ordering and purchasing goods and

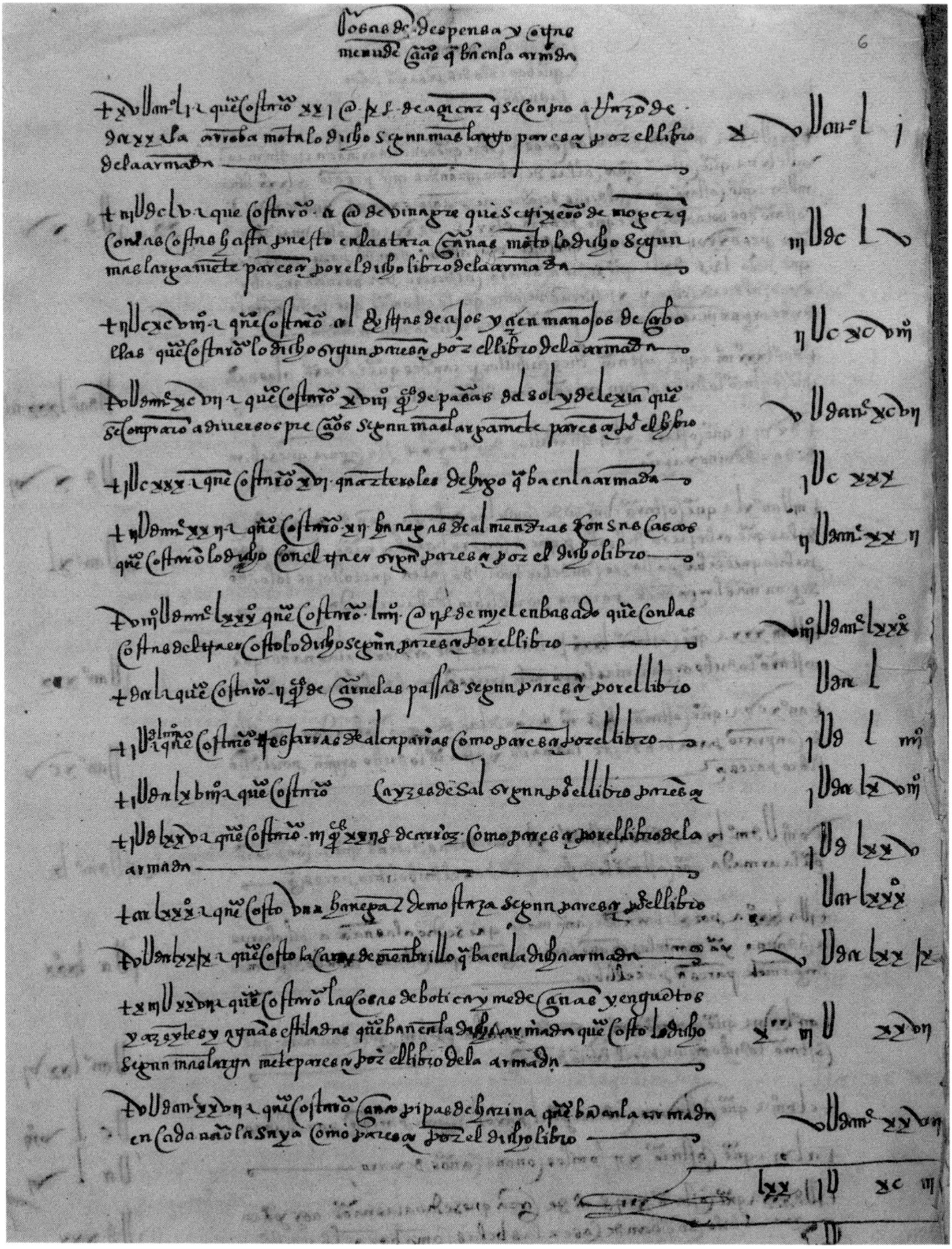

Page from the record book listing artillery and gunpowder carried on the fleet.

General Archives of the Indies, Seville

seeing to it that they were properly packed for safekeeping before being loaded onto the ships.

Tools and materials for ship repairs included hammers, anvils, pickaxes, and spades; pulleys, needles, rope, and twine. Especially important to carry on board were large quantities of canvas to replace sails that would be destroyed in storms, as well as lumber to repair hulls that would be damaged by accident or eaten away by marine worms in tropical waters.

Cooking for 270 men required large, heavy cookware. Among the stock were six cauldrons, weighing a total of 280 pounds, and five pots, weighing 132 pounds. (The unit of measure then was a quintal, which is equivalent to about 100 pounds.) There were 100 mess bowls, all that was necessary for the lot of men, since they would eat not at the same time but in shifts. There were big iron ladles for serving, but no forks or knives. The men would eat with their hands.

Fishing gear included chain hooks, cord, harpoons, and spears, and 10,500 fishhooks. Records show that amid the storeroom cargo were eighty-nine lanterns for nights with little or no moonlight, and eighteen *ampolettas*, hourglasses, to be turned by grummets, or ships' boys, every half hour, the only means of telling time.

Magellan knew from other seafarers who had sailed in pursuit of conquest and riches that it would be wise to bring gifts to give and trade with island natives in order to win their friendship and cooperation. The articles that Europeans had offered in the past were trinkets of little value to them at home. But islanders were fascinated by novelties made of materials they had never seen before, such as brass and copper. Arrangements were made for Magellan's fleet to carry thousands of bracelets and small bells, as well as mirrors, knives, and scissors (as many as fifty dozen pairs). Bolts of various colored cloths, red caps, hair combs, and assorted beads were also stocked.

PROVISIONS

Magellan wanted to insure good health and high spirits among the crews, so he insisted upon substantial food rations. Since drying and salting were the only methods of preserving meat and fish, large amounts were ordered and prepared. Included on the lists were:

6,060 pounds salt pork	4,700 pounds olive oil
200 barrels sardines	21,120 pounds cheese
238 bundles dried codfish	1,700 pounds dried fish in barrels
21,383 pounds biscuit, called hardtack	7 cows and 3 pigs to slaughter

415 casks of wine from Jerez

hundreds of pounds each of dried beans and peas, lentils, onions, honey, sugar, raisins, currants, olives, figs, and almonds

Navigation Instruments

Among the listed cargo were:

6 wooden quadrants	15 bronze-fitted wooden quadrants
6 metal astrolabes	12 compasses and 37 compass needles
23 nautical charts	13 anchors

18 sand-filled hourglasses (12 were purchased by Magellan)

Artillery and Firearms

Most artillery was secured from Spain's foundry city of Bilbao. The flagship was the only vessel armed with cannon; four were mounted on gun carriages. Her broadside artillery consisted of twenty muzzle-loading brass or iron bombards. When they were lit by flame, they shot iron or stone balls. Light artillery discharged a shower of pebbles, nails, and bits of scrap iron for short-range use. Magellan secured matchlock harquebuses—muzzle-loading musket firearms newly devised by the Turks.

60 crossbows	360 dozen arrows
95 dozen darts	20 dozen steel-headed javelins
1,000 lances	200 pikes
3 tons of gunpowder	cannonballs of iron and stone
100 steel corselets with armlets and shoulder plates	100 helmets
100 breastplates with throat pieces	200 shields

Records of all provisions were carefully kept, but Magellan's enemies conspired to disrupt the enterprise with false counts of foodstuffs and by shortchanging the amounts loaded on board. This sabotage was instigated by none other than Portugal's King Manuel, who had flown into a rage upon hearing of Magellan's plan to sail under the Spanish flag. Of course, this was the same plan that he had turned down earlier, causing Magellan to leave his court.

King Manuel now ordered a Portuguese agent in Spain, Sebastião Álvares, to stir up as much trouble as possible for Magellan. The agent not only schemed to shortchange the stores on board, he also urged the fleet pilots, the most essential crewmen for navigation, to refuse to put to sea altogether, reminding them that they didn't know precisely where the journey would take them. This caused more unrest among the crew. The agent, hoping to assure Manuel that the enterprise would end in failure, wrote him a letter saying that the ships were "very old and patched up" and had "ribs as soft as butter."

To make matters worse, Faleiro was becoming increasingly distant and temperamental. It was said he was teetering on the edge of madness and was not expected to make the voyage at all. Eventually, that is what happened. As later reported, the mathematician and astronomer who had helped to encourage Magellan and his plan ended up in an institution for the mad.

As for the ever-scheming Bishop Fonseca, he approached King Charles one last time and tried to convince him that Magellan was not trustworthy and should not be put in full command. But Charles remained steadfastly loyal to Magellan as he grew more and more to share Magellan's vision. In fact, friendship between the two deepened. Besides, Charles had become more powerful than ever. In addition to his role as king of Spain, he had been named emperor of the Holy Roman Empire, and now took the new name of Charles V.

Meanwhile, the cost of preparing the fleet was mounting—far beyond what the king was willing to sanction. Maritime house records show amounts that included purchase of the ships and longboats, materials for rigging, labor for reconditioning, and piloting charges on the river from Cádiz to Seville, totaling 2,716,589 maravedis, equivalent to $290,675 in today's money. To cover last-minute expenses Charles finally allowed Haro and a handful of other businessmen to invest in the voyage.

After months and months of preparation and delays, Charles was growing impatient. He decided to announce a departure date, and he named August 10, 1519. With that he also sent a royal order to the crew. He advised good conduct and requested that the men not swear or play cards or dice, because such actions would give rise to "evil, scandal, and strife." He also counseled the men to behave kindly toward native peoples they met and to actively win their friendship.

Throughout the preparations Magellan had managed to keep the details of his destination secret. However, close to departure time he gave Charles a confidential memorandum in which he noted the latitudes and positions of the Spice Islands, according to the best of his knowledge.

For himself Magellan prepared a last will and testament. He began, "I, Hernando de Magallanes, Comendador, His Majesty's Captain-General of the Armada bound for the Spice Islands, husband of Beatriz Barbosa, and inhabitant of this most noble and loyal city of Seville . . . being well and in good health, and possessed of such of my ordinary senses and judgment as God our Lord has, of His mercy and will, thought fit and right to endow me; believing firmly and truly in the Holy Trinity, the Father, Son, and Holy Ghost—as every faithful Christian holds and believes . . ." He went on to ask that God "have compassion and pity upon [Magellan's soul] and redeem and save it, and bring it to His glory and His heavenly Kingdom."

Magellan then made bequests to his wife, his infant son, Rodrigo, who had been born during the past year, and to an unborn child whom his wife was carrying. Magellan's brother, sister, Enrique, and Cristovão Rebêlo were also provided a sum. Magellan made further bequests to several monasteries and asked that twelve masses be said for him yearly at the altar of the Lord Jesus in the Church of San Salvador in Sabrosa.

Finally, Magellan prepared to depart. He bade his wife farewell and, on the Sunday before departure, gathered with the crew and their families for High Mass in the Church of Santa María de la Victoria de Triana, near the dockyard. Flags and banners adorned the church outside, and cannon thundered. Inside, the tone was solemn and serious. Magellan and the highest fleet officers knelt on the altar steps and swore an oath of allegiance to King Charles. The officers then vowed obedience to Magellan and swore to "follow the course ordered by him and to obey him in everything."

Of course, the three Spanish captains, who had been turned against Magellan, had no intention of obeying their commander. In fact, they were already plotting to kill him once they put to sea.

On August 10, as scheduled, the fleet hoisted anchor and set out for the harbor at Seville. They sailed down the Guadalquivir River toward the ocean port of Sanlúcar de Barrameda, a distance of some fifty-seven miles. But as soon as they reached the port, Magellan discovered the shortage of food. Angry, but not disheartened, he ordered the longboats back to Seville to pick up missing supplies.

That took another full month. At long last, after that latest and most frustrating delay, Magellan's voyage began. But as the captain-general set forth with faith and trust in his enterprise, he was actually surrounded by enemies and spies.

CHAPTER FIVE
The Voyage Begins

It was Tuesday, September 20, 1519. The five ships weighed anchor and hoisted their sails. The wind filled the sails, and Magellan's fleet gathered way.

Antonio Pigafetta, sailing on the *Trinidad*, began his journal. It is this journal that gives us the voyage's most detailed observations.

At the outset Pigafetta described the captain-general as a "wise and virtuous man and mindful of his honor." With so many perils and uncertainties at sea, it was necessary for captains-general to maintain strict order and discipline. Pigafetta, as well as all mariners, understood that only a man of exceptionally strong leadership could be in command.

Magellan established firm regulations from the start. He required all ships to approach his flagship every evening at dusk. The captains were to salute him, and he would then give sailing orders for that night and the following day. In the dark the fleet would communicate by lighted torch or lantern. If trouble was sighted, like shoals or reefs that might cause a ship to go aground, a cannon was to be fired. Everyone was obliged to join in daily prayer.

Pages were to take four-hour shifts turning the sand clocks. There were three night periods, referred to as "first watch," "sleepy watch," and "dawn watch." Each shift change was to be accompanied by a prayer or psalm recitation, to assure the officers that the boy on duty was fully awake. Sometimes a cabin boy would sing a little ditty, like:

> *On deck, gentlemen of the starboard watch,*
> *Hurry and get up, get up!*

By necessity food was rationed. Cooking would take place on deck and only in favorable weather. Even then, it needed to be done cautiously on the leeward side of the ship, away from the wind, so that sparks or flames would blow outward and be less likely to start a fire. Buckets of water were always kept close at hand.

All expeditions that departed Spain made for the Canary Islands to take on more water and wood before venturing farther into the Atlantic. The islands were not far, but that is where Magellan's troubles at sea began. While they were at Tenerife, the capital, Magellan received an urgent message delivered by a ship dispatched from Spain. The message was written by his father-in-law, Diogo Barbosa, and it warned Magellan to watch for his safety. Barbosa had learned that Magellan's life was in danger. The three Spanish captains, led by Juan de Cartagena, were plotting to kill him as soon as they left the Canaries.

Magellan took the warning in stride and remained on guard while he figured out a strategy to defeat the plot. When the time came to depart, he gave sailing orders for a southerly course along the west coast of Africa. But the captains argued for a southwesterly course. Magellan agreed with their decision because he was aware that they could easily overpower him as soon as they reached a distance from land. Then, in the midst of the agreed route, Magellan suddenly changed course. The scheming captains were thrown into confusion. They had no choice but to follow the captain-general, or they would be left behind. Magellan had outwitted them and caused them to lose their opportunity, at least for the moment. He had sent a strong message with his quick action. He remained firmly in command.

Magellan had realized that Bishop Fonseca was behind the plot. He also suspected that King Manuel's ships were lying in wait nearby, ready to attack. Magellan was right about his suspicions, and when he veered off the originally planned course, he had made a wise move.

For some time the fleet sailed in good weather and fair winds. But two weeks later the ships met their first tropical storms. Violent gales and headwinds lashed at them, tossing them wildly hour after hour and leaving many terrified men aboard weeping and praying.

Suddenly, the sailors saw an amazing sight—great, bright sparks flashing on the mastheads. The lights were "like blazing torches shining so brightly on the topsail that we were blinded," Pigafetta wrote. There is no indication that the men had seen or heard of such flashes before, and like many people in Magellan's time, the sailors were superstitious. The sight of something unexplainable was terrifying.

Then they began to wonder. Perhaps the flashes were divine lights sent by Saint Elmo, the patron saint of mariners, who had come to protect them. Once they convinced themselves of this, they began to feel a sense of calm and comfort. The flashes later came to be understood as electrical charges that occur in a storm. We call the phenomenon St. Elmo's fire.

Soon afterward the fleet found itself trapped in doldrums, where almost no winds stirred at all. The ships had reached the equatorial zone. They could do nothing but drift for three weeks, as the sailors suffered from stifling heat, hunger, and thirst. The conditions were unbearable.

Finally, a slight wind came up. It gradually increased, until they entered the belt of southeast trade winds. On November 20, sailing southwesterly, the fleet crossed the equator. They had reached the southern hemisphere of the world. At nightfall, when the sailors looked skyward, they were awestruck. There in the southern sky was a constellation most of them had never seen.

The wondrous sight was the Southern Cross. It would now become their navigational guide. Earlier, they had been guided by

St. Elmo's fire. NORTH WIND PICTURE ARCHIVES

the position of the Pole Star (North Star), but when they crossed the equator, the North Star vanished.

Magellan steered the armada south southwest in steady trade winds, but currents set the true course southwest by west. A week later they approached Brazil. The master's mate on the *Trinidad*, a Greek named Francisco Albo who later would become a pilot, began a navigation logbook on that date, November 29. The log has survived and has proved invaluable to historians.

On December 8 Albo recorded that the *Trinidad* reached latitude 19° S when she raised land and found bottom. Magellan feared making landfall there because that region of Brazil belonged to Portugal, and the fleet was in Portuguese waters. But the fleet needed to replenish supplies. Instead, they sailed farther south southwest and finally due west until they arrived at a hospitable and beautiful harbor, Guanabara Bay, which earlier explorers also called Rio de Janeiro. Unaware of that name, Magellan called it Bahía Santa Lucía in honor of the saint they celebrated that day, December 13. Some historians believe that this bay was probably where Magellan was heading when he sailed from the Canary Islands.

The people there had long suffered a drought, but it rained on the day the fleet arrived. Believing that the strange visitors had brought the rain, the inhabitants joyfully welcomed them and gladly exchanged items like pineapples and sweet potatoes and colorful parrots for the trinkets the visitors offered. They even happily traded six plump chickens for a single playing card—a king.

While Albo recorded navigational information on position,

NORTH

Spain

Canary
Islands

AFRICA

Cape Verde
Islands

equator

ATLANTIC
OCEAN

Brazil

SOUTH
AMERICA

Rio de Janeiro

Argentina

San Julián

Tierra
del Fuego

WEST

EAST

MAGELLAN
IN THE
ATLANTIC

SOUTH

winds, distance runs, and courses, the chronicler Pigafetta filled his journal with observations about people and their manners and customs. Studies now tell us that the people of that region were probably Tupi or Guaraní tribes. Pigafetta described them as olive toned and wrote that they went about naked, lived in harmony with nature, slept in communal houses, and made boats from a tree—all in one piece—which they called canoes. He noted that they were not Christians, but they might "be easily converted."

Brazil was a paradise for the European sailors. With seasons reversed south of the equator, they basked in the summer sun of December and January of the new year, 1520. They enjoyed healthful foods and delighted in the delicate scent of flowers and fruit blossoms carried on balmy breezes. It didn't take long before many of them turned lazy and behaved poorly. Some disobeyed orders and even ran off for days at a time.

It was in this atmosphere that the rebels decided once more to

---

Years earlier, while he was in Portuguese service, the pilot João Lopes Carvalho had lived and traded in Brazil, and he had learned the language well enough to act as translator. At Pigafetta's urging, Lopes Carvalho taught the chronicler many useful words. Pigafetta recorded some of them in his journal:

pinda — fishhook	*taisse* — knife	*pirame* — scissors
huy — flour	*chiquap* — comb	*iteumaraca* — bell
maiz — millet	*tum* — good	*maragatum* — better

---

act. Juan de Cartagena organized several men to undermine the captain-general's command by refusing to salute him. Magellan recognized that another mutiny plot was under way. Again he wisely took action first. One night at the right moment, he seized Cartagena by surprise in his cabin, calmly announcing, "Rebel, this is mutiny. In the name of the king, you are my prisoner."

When Magellan started to lock the prisoner in chains, the other traitorous captains, Gaspar de Quesada and Luis de Mendoza, begged for their friend's release. Worried about Cartagena's close relationship to the Spanish court and the condemnation he himself might suffer, Magellan decided to hand his prisoner over to the *Victoria* for close watch and replaced him with another captain. This captain proved to be unworthy, so he was replaced with a distant cousin of Magellan's, Álvaro de Mesquita. In the next change of officers, Magellan named *Concepción* pilot João Lopes Carvalho as pilot on the flagship *Trinidad*, since he was familiar with Brazil's coastal waters.

With renewed confidence Magellan now prepared to push forward. He was especially eager to do so because Brazil's coast veered westward, and the farther south they sailed, the sooner they would be on the other side of the line of demarcation and thus in Spanish territorial waters. He was even more eager to find the passage that would take him from the Atlantic Ocean to the other great sea. Magellan believed that *el paso* lay nearby, at about latitude 35° S.

In the middle of January the fleet approached a cape that lay at the latitude Magellan had anticipated. There appeared to be a channel, too. What great fortune! Magellan chose that moment to reveal his knowledge of the passage to the men, who still had not been told of the enterprise's destination. They were all happily surprised, and their hopes were raised high.

Magellan ordered the *Santiago* ahead to explore the channel, while he awaited good news. The caravel returned earlier than expected, however. And the news was bad. The channel water was not salty ocean water. It was freshwater, and the channel was only a river (now known as Río de la Plata in Buenos Aires). Magellan was stunned. How could this be? He was badly shaken, yet the tough, resolute man who never accepted defeat composed himself and continued a southward course. He did not know it, but he was heading toward the South Pole, in the uninhabitable frozen land of the Antarctic.

By now it was February. In the southern hemisphere, that meant winter would soon be approaching. A powerful storm struck, bringing thunder, lightning, and gales that drove the ships toward sandbanks again and again. All five ships were terribly battered. Raw hunger overcame the seamen. It was not until they "discovered two islands full of geese and goslings and sea wolves," as Pigafetta wrote, that they could get fresh provisions, which they did by killing and cooking the "geese." Pigafetta described them as "black with feathers over their whole body" and observed that they "do not fly." These sea birds were penguins. The sea wolves of "various colors and of the size and thickness of a calf have large teeth and no legs, but they have feet attached to their body and resembling a human hand. If they could run they would be 'fierce and cruel,' but they do not leave the water." These creatures were fur seals, a species that lives only in Arctic and Antarctic regions and was not familiar to Europeans.

The weather grew worse. When the fleet reached latitude 45° S, the first cold blast from the Antarctic struck with ferocity. Blinding fog made it nearly impossible for the pilots to navigate. The seamen, in wet, icy clothes, suffered raw, stinging hands and feet. They feared freezing to death. They begged Magellan to go back to Brazil.

Magellan suffered a fear worse than ice and cold. What would happen if he returned to Spain empty-handed? It would mean certain ruin for him. He would probably be sent to prison, too. He refused to hear the frantic cries of the men and instead led the fleet in a desperate search for refuge in a sheltered anchorage, where he intended they would stay until spring, nearly six months later.

At the end of March 1520, the five beaten ships managed to make their way to a bay on the coast of Argentina. Magellan named it Bahía San Julián, in honor of Saint Julián. The exhausted crews were relieved to have rest, a freshwater supply, and fish, which they cooked over wood fires. They set about reconditioning the ships. There was no need to hurry, so they took their time doing the work.

Everyone appeared contented. But Magellan knew otherwise. He was well aware of the whispers and grumblings behind his back. Once again his enemies were preparing to strike. This time, however, Magellan was unable to prevent mutiny.

Magellanic penguins, a species native to Patagonia. Courtesy of Arthur Arnold

In the black of night, before Easter Sunday, Juan de Cartagena and Gaspar de Quesada stealthily climbed aboard the *San Antonio* and seized the newly named captain, the loyal Álvaro de Mesquita. They chained him and locked him up, and after that they took hold of three Portuguese sailors. The crew heard the scuffle and rushed on deck. As soon as they gathered, the mutinous leaders urged them all to join their revolt.

Just then the ship's master, Juan de Elorriaga, another officer loyal to Magellan, stepped forward and shouted to the mutineers, "I demand in the name of God and King Charles that you return to your ship. I also demand that you release our captain." No sooner had Elorriaga finished speaking than Quesada swiftly thrust a dagger into him, fatally wounding him. With that, the crew of forty found itself at the mercy of the mutineers.

Then, in order to win the crew over to their cause, Cartagena and Quesada opened the food lockers and let the men grab what they could without any rationing. It did not take long before the entire crew of forty agreed to join the uprising.

Cartagena took charge of the *Concepción* and sent the ship's master, Juan Sebastián del Cano (called Elcano or Cano), to help Quesada on the *San Antonio*. The third traitorous captain, Luis de Mendoza, remained in command of the *Victoria*.

All of this had taken place in the middle of the night, and the rest of the fleet did not discover the treachery until dawn. Magellan was both furious and alarmed. Three ships were now in the hands of mutineers. Nevertheless, the staunch captain-general resolved to put down the uprising. When the leaders presented him with a note of demands, he feigned a show of goodwill and invited them aboard the *Trinidad* to discuss the matter. Meanwhile, he hastily prepared several faithful men, including the flagship's master-at-arms, who had proved himself strong and steadfast to Magellan from the outset. His name was Gonzalo Gómez de Espinosa.

The instant Mendoza stepped aboard, Espinosa brutally stabbed him to death. At the same time, fifteen heavily armed men sneaked onto the *San Antonio* by way of a longboat, and from there they managed to overtake the *Victoria*, shouting, "Long live the emperor! Death to the traitors!"

Magellan next ordered the *Trinidad*, *Victoria*, and *Santiago*, captained by João Serrão, to block the harbor and trap the still-mutineer-controlled *San Antonio* and *Concepción*. The traitors were seized, chained, and put below deck. The uprising was over.

A court-martial was held, and all traitors were found guilty of mutiny. According to the custom of maritime rule, the penalty for mutiny was death. Often, further cruel measures were ordered. Luis de Mendoza, already dead from stabbing, was quartered and decapitated. Gaspar de Quesada met the same fate.

Juan de Cartagena was spared for the time being because he was related to Bishop Fonseca, whose influence at court Magellan feared. Cartagena was confined to ship's quarters. That did not stop him from continuing to plot against Magellan, however. When Magellan learned this, he decided upon another gruesome yet common maritime punishment. He ordered Cartagena and a French chaplain, Cartagena's latest accomplice in scheming, to be marooned on an island and left with nothing but their swords, a supply of wine, and some biscuits. Their fate is unknown.

The *San Antonio* crew were also found guilty of treason, but officers pleaded for their pardon because all hands were needed on deck to work. Admitting this, Magellan commuted their death sentences and ordered them to hard labor doing the worst drudgery, like cleaning the filthy bilges where the ship's wastes collected. All the while they were chained at the ankles. Among those was Juan Sebastián del Cano, who later would become, after Magellan, the best-known figure in the story of the first circumnavigation of the globe.

According to Maximilian of Transylvania, a court observer who lived during the time, Magellan was rightfully enraged by the traitorous leaders, but his chosen penalties were perhaps "more harsh than was proper for a foreigner, especially when commanding in a distant country." On the other hand, the observer understood that Magellan had "made up his mind either to die or to complete his enterprise."

With the bloody deeds done, Magellan pushed the fleet forward. He dispatched the *Santiago* ahead to explore. Sixty nautical miles south southwest of San Julián, Captain João Serrão discovered a long, deep estuary, which he named Santa Cruz. By now it was May, and at that latitude, winter was approaching. The caravel first met heavy headwinds. Then, suddenly, she was struck badly by a strong squall, and hard as the crew fought, the ship was cast ashore. The *Santiago* was shipwrecked.

With broken timbers the men built a raft, and two sailors made their way back to San Julián in freezing conditions, arriving eleven days later. The wretched fellows were so emaciated and frostbitten that they were not recognized at first. Immediately, Magellan sent a rescue party with bread and wine for the others at Santa Cruz, but sailing conditions were so treacherous that the men had to walk along the rugged shore. It remains unknown how the shipwreck victims and their rescuers returned. It's believed that they traveled overland and arrived the third week of July.

Back at San Julián, the rescued crew was divided among the four remaining ships. Mesquita continued as captain of the *San Antonio*.

Magellan. THE MARINERS' MUSEUM, NEWPORT NEWS, VIRGINIA

Serrão, whose caravel was shipwrecked, was put in charge of the *Concepción*, and Duarte Barbosa, Diogo Barbosa's son and Magellan's brother-in-law, was named captain of the *Victoria*.

All together, the miserable ordeal of waiting at San Julián lasted five months. Provisions were pitifully low. The only available fresh food was mussels. There were large ostrichlike birds, believed to be rheas (also called nandus), and big rodents nearby; however, the men had difficulty hunting them. The bitter, intense cold never let up. Several men perished.

One day toward the end of their stay a visitor showed up, surprising everyone, since no inhabitants of the region had appeared in all that time. Pigafetta described the man as "a giant . . . who danced, leaped, and sang. He had a very large face, painted round with yellow, and in the middle of his cheeks he had two hearts painted. . . . [H]e was clad in the skin of a certain animal, which skin was very skillfully sewn together." The animal was the guanaco, a relative of the llama unfamiliar to European visitors in South America.

Soon other natives appeared, painted with different designs and all described as extremely large in size. Magellan called them "Patagones"—from *pata de cano*, possibly because their hide-wrapped feet looked like dogs' paws. They would become known as Patagonians and the region as Patagonia. Later explorers and travelers also described giant-sized men and women there, but no conclusive evidence exists that they were "giants." The people are believed to have been Tehuelche Indians, probably taller and heavier than the Europeans.

Magellan and the Europeans found them so curious that they captured two men by playing a cruel trick on them. Seeing that the men admired ship wares that were made of iron, which was unfamiliar to the Indians, they filled the mens' hands with heavy objects and then "showed them" how to carry more iron on their legs. Those items turned out to be leg irons that were immediately locked around their ankles. As soon as the innocent men realized that they had been tricked, they "raged like bulls, calling for their god to help them," as Pigafetta described the scene. Tragically, they were forced aboard, and both eventually died. Tehuelche Indians are now virtually extinct.

It was not until August that the fierce storms let up and the fleet was able to depart for Santa Cruz, the estuary where the shipwreck had occurred. There they anchored and laid in a fresh supply of fish, game, seals, and sea birds, which they salted and smoked. They stayed until everyone was satisfied that the provisions were plentiful enough to last for some time.

Southern spring blossomed in October. The men were thankful for calm and sunny weather and prepared to depart. Finally, one morning, they gathered to recite High Mass. Then the ships weighed anchor and put to sea. Magellan fervently prayed that he would find *el paso* soon.

CHAPTER SIX
Destined for Danger

Magellan did not actually know whether a seaway passage existed or not. But he was so determined to find one that he refused to listen to the qualms and fears of his men, and he closed his mind to any doubts of his own. Instead, against strong, punishing headwinds, he led the fleet still farther south, to a long sandy point he named Cape Vírgenes, in honor of Saint Ursula, on whose birthday, October 21, it was discovered. (It is now Point Dungeness.)

Pilot Albo logged the position at latitude 52° S. Soon afterward they came to a bay that extended deep inland; Magellan anchored the *Trinidad* and the *Victoria* there and dispatched the *San Antonio* and the *Concepción* to investigate.

Without warning, a great tempest struck, causing the anchored ships to roll and pitch without letup for two days. Inside the bay the raging gales tossed the reconnaissance ships about until the *San Antonio* managed to take shelter in a cove. Unexpectedly, the cove appeared to lead toward a channel. The *Concepción*, which had been forced through a narrows, also discovered something unusual. The tidal current was especially strong; the water was salty; a depth sounding indicated a deep channel without sandbars. Could *this* be the sea passage that Magellan was seeking? Did a strait really exist, after all?

Magellan waited in suspense. Finally, four days later, as Pigafetta recorded, "[W]e saw the two ships approaching under full sail and

Discovery of the strait. THE MARINERS' MUSEUM, NEWPORT NEWS, VIRGINIA

flying their banners. We joyously greeted them and all thanked God and the Virgin Mary." Álvaro de Mesquita, in command on the *San Antonio*, cried out to Magellan, "Hail, my captain-general. I have the honor to report the discovery of *el paso*."

Magellan rejoiced and prepared to go forward as soon as possible. There were important questions to consider, though. How seaworthy were the four remaining ships? Were there enough provisions? Would there be more mutinous uprisings? Magellan answered each in good faith, resolute to continue the mission he believed to be his destiny. "Even if we have to eat the leather wrappings on the masts and yards, I will still go on to discover what I have promised Our Lord the King," he announced, "and I trust that God will aid us and give us good fortune."

At dawn on October 21, 1520, the fleet entered the eastern mouth of the passage. As Magellan and his men were to learn, this was no easy, direct route. They were embarking on a long, dangerous course of winding channels in a hostile region of rough seas, icy fog, and howling winds. For days they passed a great expanse of land with a wondrous span of snowcapped mountains rising in the background. At nightfall they saw fires in the distance and understood that they were built by natives in remote villages. Magellan named this region Tierra del Fuego, which means Land of Fire.

Beyond that region, they found themselves surrounded by altogether different terrains: first, rain-drenched forests and then level plains covered with moss, ferns, and stunted trees. Days later they made their way through a narrows that veered southwest. Soon

Headlands of Tierra del Fuego. North Wind Picture Archives

they passed yet another landscape, one of green and brown rolling fields. These were awesome sights indeed.

Three centuries later, British scientist Charles Darwin would describe the passage as "an endless succession of gales . . . rapid, turbulent, and unconfined atmospheric currents," yet with a waterway that followed "like a river in its bed, a regularly determined course."

Pigafetta wrote, "[T]here is not a more beautiful or better strait in the world." No matter how breathtaking, the strait of unknown waters, with its twists and turns and narrow channels, was a treacherous place to maneuver, especially in the dark of the night. In years to follow, mariners from all over the world marveled at Ferdinand Magellan's extraordinary skills in navigating such a course for its entire length—334 miles.

Sailing south past a place now called Punta Arenas, they arrived at an island that divided the strait. One channel turned southwest and the other southeast. Magellan sent the *San Antonio* and *Concepción* southeast to explore, while he remained with the *Victoria* near a river that would supply the fleet with a large quantity of sardines. All agreed to meet again in a few days.

Magellan happened upon a wide and straight channel. This was significant indeed. Without delay he sent the *Trinidad*'s longboat forward. The sailors rowed mightily against powerful tides; several days later they returned, exclaiming, "We found it. The great South Sea!" That was all Magellan had longed to hear. He wept with joy.

In all that time the *San Antonio* had failed to return. Magellan and the men waited impatiently, occupying themselves by catching sardines and sea birds to cook and preserve. After a week had gone by, their worry turned to fear. Had the *San Antonio* disappeared or met with an accident? Had magical powers been cast over the ship? Had traitorous enemies aboard forced her to return to Spain, where wicked rumors would be spread about Magellan? After a desperate search, no trace of the ship was found. That meant a serious loss, for the *San Antonio* was the largest ship and carried provisions and supplies for the entire fleet.

The story of what had happened was learned later. Spanish mutineers had convinced the *San Antonio*'s crew that Magellan was a

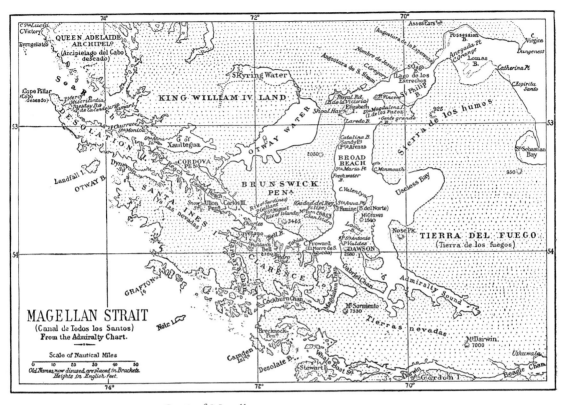

Strait of Magellan. NORTH WIND PICTURE ARCHIVES

madman and that they would all end up frozen corpses. When the loyal captain, Álvaro de Mesquita, refused to obey the demand to return to Spain, the mutineers seized him and forced him to sign a statement that Magellan had unjustly mistreated Spanish officers at San Julián. The ship then returned to the Atlantic and made its way back to Seville, arriving six months later. The officers were arrested but released soon afterward. Spanish authorities didn't believe Mesquita's explanation of what had happened. Bishop

Fonseca was enraged to find out that Juan de Cartagena, his son, had been marooned on an island and left to die and ordered Mesquita to prison. Eventually, Mesquita was released and returned to his home in Portugal.

With the *San Antonio* gone three ships remained. Magellan made ready to complete the journey through the passage. Still worrying about criticism back in Spain, he prepared documents in defense of his actions after the San Julián mutiny and stated his resolve to continue the voyage. "I understand that all of you consider it a grave matter that I am determined to go forward, for it appears to you that there is little time for completing the voyage," he wrote. "As I am a man who never scorns the opinion and counsel of anyone, all my decisions are put into practice and communicated generally to everyone so that no one need feel affronted." He also promised that God would see them through to the successful conclusion of their quest.

Magellan urged the captains, as well as other officers, to put their opinions in writing. Even though they were terrified to go on, they couldn't forget the bloody scenes after the Easter week uprising at San Julián. In the end they bowed to Magellan's wishes. One wrote, "I believe that our Grace should go forward while we have the flower of summer in hand, to continue our exploration until the middle of January." Magellan's statement and the men's letters were copied into a notebook by one of the officers and were signed and sealed on November 21, 1520.

Magellan ordered the anchors lifted, and the *Trinidad, Concepción,*

A version of the South American region near the seaway passage, as illustrated by a mapmaker several decades after Magellan's voyage. NORTH WIND PICTURE ARCHIVES and *Victoria* sailed out of the western gateway of the passage. He named the passage the Strait of All Saints. It is now called the Strait of Magellan. The strait lies north of Cape Horn and separates Tierra del Fuego from the mainland of South America.

After thirty-eight days in that treacherous seaway, on November 28, 1520, the men spotted a rocky headland, and they heard the roar of the ocean. Stretching ahead of Magellan and his fleet lay the Great South Sea.

CHAPTER SEVEN

The Endless Ocean

"Gentlemen, we now are steering into waters where no ship has sailed before," Magellan told his men. "May we always find them as peaceful as they are this morning. In this hope I shall name this sea the Mar Pacífico [Peaceful Ocean]. Set sail. Follow me!"

The men raised banners, fired bombards, and sang hymns in praise of the Almighty. With renewed excitement the fleet gathered way once more. Ferdinand Magellan was about to become the first European to explore the Pacific Ocean. But on that momentous day, when he set forth, could he or any of his men have had any idea of what truly lay ahead?

It wasn't long before doubts and suspicions rose again. On the first night out the dark sky revealed a strange celestial sight—cloudy patches of light. Today we know them as the Magellanic Clouds, which are seen in the southern sky and recognized as galaxies neighboring our own, the Milky Way. But long ago they were a mystery. Earlier in the voyage the superstitious sailors had believed that flashes of light on the masts during a storm protected them. Now, however, they viewed this new sight as an omen of troubles to come.

The fleet steered north along the coast and then headed westward into the open sea, with agreeable winds at their back. According to pilot Albo's log, which traced the Pacific Ocean voyage, Magellan "could hardly have shaped a better course. He avoided dangerous island-studded waters and made the best use of prevailing winds and currents." The favorable conditions continued for two weeks, and fears and doubts subsided. Anticipation was high once more. Magellan assured his crew that they would reach the Moluccas soon.

But then a week passed. Two weeks. Three weeks. Still there was no sign of the islands. Magellan altered course. By now the weary seafarers' dreams of reaching the Moluccas began to fade. The men grew irritable. Their tempers flared. They argued and fought. Often there were explosions of violence. With food supplies dwindling rapidly, rations became stricter. The wine was gone. The water putrefied. The ocean was far greater in width than Magellan or any explorer or mapmaker had imagined.

On February 13, they crossed the equator again, this time heading north. The blazing sun and sweltering heat were excruciating. So was the gnawing ache of hunger. The only food they had left was smoked penguin meat, but it had long since rotted. Worms

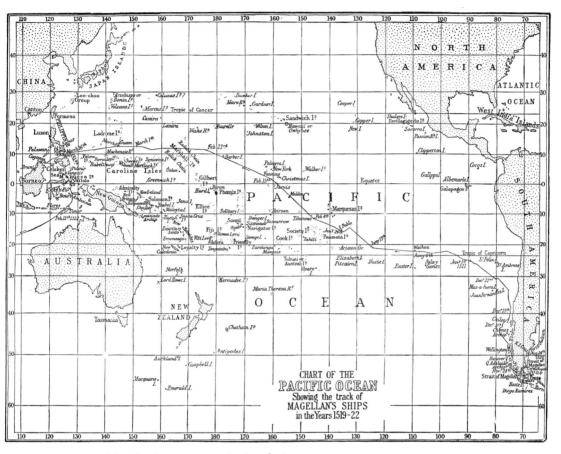

Magellan's route across the Pacific Ocean. North Wind Picture Archives

bred in the spoiled meat and crawled everywhere, eating their way through woolen clothing and even leather goods.

Would these miseries never end? Pigafetta wrote: "We ate biscuit that was no longer biscuit, but powder of biscuits, swarming with worms. They stank strongly of rats' urine. We also ate certain ox hides that covered the tops of the yards to keep them from chafing the shrouds, and which had become exceedingly hard because of the sun, rain, and wind. We soaked them in the sea for four or five days, and then placed them briefly on hot ashes, and so we ate them; often we ate sawdust." Could Magellan ever have imagined how prophetic his words would be when he had earlier vowed to eat the leather wrappings on the masts and yards?

The men became so desperate that they resorted to bargaining with each other for any scrap they could get their hands on. "Rats were sold for half a ducat apiece, and even so, we could not always get them," Pigafetta continued. "But above all the other misfortunes, the worst was that the gums of the lower and upper teeth of some of our men swelled, so that they could not eat and they died of hunger."

The agonizing syndrome that caused swollen gums was part of the worst suffering that befell the sailors, a medical condition that was not wholly understood at the time. Not only did the gums swell and bleed, but if a stricken man tried to eat, his teeth would fall out. He also suffered agonizing body sores, swollen joints, and bleeding from the nose and mouth. The illness is called "scurvy." Without ascorbic acid, another term for vitamin C, from fresh fruits and vegetables, a body develops these symptoms. During the age of exploration Magellan and other voyagers knew that reaching land and eating the fresh fruit that it yielded helped cure the sick and prevented the disease in others. Oddly, some men fell ill with scurvy and others did not, so the true cause remained a mystery until two centuries later.

Some historians have wondered about the reason for Magellan's continued good health. Was it because he kept a supply of quince jelly in his cabin? Since it is still not medically understood why some people contract certain diseases and others do not, it is difficult to speculate.

Magellan was reported to have helped minister to the ill throughout the ordeal. When nothing was left from which to make a broth, he used bits of biscuits, including maggots, for nourishment. He even scraped casks that had held food, as well as slivers of barrel sawdust, to make into a thin gruel. He asked the dying and the most feeble if they had keepsakes that he might take back to their families.

Magellan was said to be "at one with his men," since he endured the hardships alongside them and never complained. True, he was a harsh and ruthless commander, a man who preferred solitude, and a "knotted and intricate" soul, as one writer has called him, but he was also a man of his time and, in the end, a hero of his age.

For two months the ships sailed across the seemingly endless ocean. Illness and death claimed the men one by one. Every few days a corpse was buried at sea. By the first of March, nineteen men were dead and twenty-five gravely ill.

Finally, on January 24, they sighted land. Unfortunately, it was of little comfort. The fleet couldn't make a landfall because there was no water shallow enough for anchorage and they could not send longboats ashore because the water was shark-infested. Moreover, there turned out to be only "two small, uninhabited islands,"

Pigafetta noted, "where we found only birds and trees, wherefore we called them the Unfortunate Isles" (now identified as Puka Puka).

Then, on the morning of March 6, 1521, a ship's boy on lookout duty shouted that he saw a dim light. Soon afterward he sighted rising peaks of two islands. At last, after three months and five days on the Pacific Ocean, the fleet of feeble, desperate seamen made landfall on a fertile island. "If our Lord and the Virgin Mother had not aided us by giving good weather to refresh ourselves with provisions," wrote Pigafetta, "we would have died in this very great sea. I believe that never more will any man undertake to make such a voyage."

But the joy and relief didn't last long. Suddenly, knife-wielding islanders with painted faces appeared in swift-sailing boats, which were described as resembling "dolphins, jumping from wave to wave." These were outrigger canoes, fitted with sails made of palm leaves sewn together and powered by warriors of great physical strength. In a flash they climbed onto the *Trinidad* and swarmed all over the flagship. Having never seen a sailing ship, metal instruments, or trinkets of beads, glass, or red cloth, they began snatching up these strange things in a frenzy of excitement.

The crew became frightened, and Magellan ordered deck artillery to be fired. The noise scared off the intruders, but not before they cut loose the *Trinidad*'s longboat and took it with them. The fleet could ill afford to lose the boat, because it was needed at harbors to fetch food and fresh water. Furious, Magellan led forty armed men ashore. In

Isle of Thieves, as charted by Pigafetta. His journal included twenty-three sketches.

their anger they killed seven men, injured others with arrows loosed from crossbows, and burned forty or fifty village houses as well as several canoes. They retrieved the longboat and loaded it with stolen coconuts, rice, yams, bananas, and chickens.

The captain-general had hoped for good relations with the natives upon his landing. But that was not to be. Instead, he and his mariners from afar had acted with unspeakable savagery.

Magellan called the island the Isle of Thieves. It is now named Guam, part of the Marianas Islands. The islanders were Chamorros, members of a Micronesian people.

Magellan could not allow himself to dwell on this catastrophe, just as he had not brooded on the mutinous events at San Julián. After all, the fleet had survived so far on "a sea so vast," wrote one contemporary observer, "that the human mind can barely grasp it."

CHAPTER EIGHT

Tragic Death

Despite the tragedies at sea and the disastrous encounter at the Isle of Thieves, Magellan felt triumphant in having crossed the great ocean. He knew that he had accomplished this feat by the determinations of instruments. Although they could not always give precise positions—especially regarding longitude—they still revealed the fleet's position closely enough to convince Magellan how far they had sailed. He also realized that it was possible to sail completely around the world.

But he soon found yet another cause for worry. They had gone so far over the line of demarcation that they were back in Portuguese waters again. This was alarming. After all, had Magellan not assured King Charles that the Spice Islands belonged to Spain? He put the worry out of his mind, however, and proceeded to lead the fleet west by south. A week later, on March 16, 1521, several men sighted mountains rising above the horizon. They were the mountains of Samar, as the island is still known today. Magellan called it San Lázaro, honoring Saint Lazarus. It is part of an archipelago of islands that in 1542 were named the Philippine Islands, in honor of the crown prince who became King Philip II of Spain. When the fleet anchored in a sheltered bay of a wooded island, Homonhon, Magellan planted a cross and a Spanish flag, claiming the islands for the Almighty God and King Charles. Magellan was the first European to reach this region by way of a western sea route.

The captain-general warned the men to be especially cautious with the inhabitants. This time, however, the people greeted them with open friendliness, and everyone took part in a joyful exchange of trinkets for chickens, oranges, coconuts, water, and palm wine.

The men stayed at Homonhon for several days, to allow the sick to recover and to recondition the ships. Then the fleet continued a west-by-southwest course, landing on an island called Limasawa (Mazaua) at the south end of the Leyte Gulf. There the people showed high excitement, for it turned out that Enrique spoke not only their language but also their dialect.

Even though Magellan had acquired Enrique in Malacca, historians believe that Enrique was born in the central Philippines. He had then been sold into slavery in Sumatra and taken to Malacca. If it is true that Enrique's birthplace was in the central Philippines, he was actually the first person to have circumnavigated the earth when he landed there with Magellan.

PHILIPPINES & SPICE ISLANDS

NORTH

SOUTH CHINA SEA

Philippines

Samar

Cebu

Leyte

Mactan

PHILIPPINE SEA

SULU SEA

WEST

EAST

CELEBES SEA

MOLUCCA SEA

Borneo

Ternate

Tidore

SPICE IS.

Celebes

Timor

SOUTH

Meanwhile, in the midst of this happy encounter, the Europeans and their hosts exchanged gifts and feasted on roast pork and rice served in Chinese porcelain. Afterward, hosts and visitors alike displayed national dances with pride. Magellan was overcome with joy. "I am now in the land I hoped to reach!" he exclaimed.

At the beginning of April the fleet proceeded to another island in the Philippines, Cebu. The reception at Cebu's port city was also gratifying. Humabon, the rajah or ruler of the island, appeared impressively dressed in red and purple silk finery and adorned with dazzling jewels. Humabon had been warned by a Muslim merchant to take caution with these Christian visitors, and so he acted especially kind and pleasant. As interpreter, Enrique explained their mission of peace and goodwill, while adding that his master was a captain of the greatest king in the world.

The encounter remained calm and cordial, and Magellan felt assured of good things from now on. He began to see his destiny not only as discoverer of a western sea route but also as someone else—a missionary responsible for bringing Christianity to island natives. Soon Magellan and an accompanying priest found themselves telling Humabon about their wondrous Almighty God. The rajah surprised Magellan by agreeing to accept the Christian God. Not only that, he also agreed to an immediate baptism ceremony. Others followed, including his wife. Magellan gave her a wooden doll of the Christ child as a gift.

In that age of exploration, seafaring leaders often held lofty visions of saving the souls of large numbers of non-Christians, whom they called infidels. These visionaries, like their sovereigns, hoped to expand their empires by bringing more people to pledge faith and allegiance to the explorers' own Christian lands and rulers. They believed that such gain at their initiative would win them the highest kingly praise. In the past, though, religious conversion by explorers had proved difficult. Most native peoples had resisted. For this reason, Magellan was stunned when many men and women of Cebu suddenly agreed to embrace his Christian God.

Indeed, Magellan soared so high at his initial success that he became more and more enraptured with newly found religious power. When a few people hesitated to convert, Magellan scolded them, fell to his knees, and promised that God would favor them if they accepted Christianity not out of fear but "with a good heart and for the love of God." The people listened.

With Enrique serving as interpreter, eight hundred men, women, and children were baptized in a mass ceremony on Easter Sunday, April 14, 1521. For days afterward Magellan preached while the priest reportedly baptized two thousand more people in ceremonies that were described as frenzied and out of control.

Magellan's swift success at conversion reached heights far beyond all he had ever imagined, and he seems to have been swept away by what he believed to be his own exalted powers. When that happened, he also lost his sense of judgment.

After all, he had just discovered the western sea route and for the first time in history had found that it was possible to circumnavigate the earth. His destination of the Spice Islands was now within his immediate reach. Why, then, was he unable to remain solely the accomplished navigator and explorer that he was?

What actually was taking place in Magellan's mind and soul is left open to historical question and interpretation. Was he driven by sincere, devout religious fervor? Did he dream of wondrous rewards from the king for converting infidels to worship Spain's Christian God? Did divine madness and zeal blind him to the reality of a large and diverse world? It seems that this part of Magellan's story must forever remain a mystery.

After the baptism ceremonies, Magellan's confidence continued to grow. He became so crazed with power that he declared he could even make Rajah Humabon's enemies on the nearby isle of Mactan bow to the Christian king of Spain as the land's supreme sovereign.

Mactan lies across a narrow channel from Cebu, and its ruler, Lapulapu, had long been a foe of Humabon. When Magellan made his demands on Lapulapu, the Mactan ruler refused to obey. Magellan then declared war. Both Humabon and Magellan's own men desperately tried to dissuade him, but Magellan would not listen to them. He was so driven by now that he insisted he could easily win with a tiny army of only sixty men. He stubbornly refused any help or advice.

At dawn on April 27 Magellan led three rowboats across the channel to Mactan. The tide was too low for them to land, however, and the men, who were only partially protected by armor, had to wade ashore. Lapulapu's army was there to meet them, and they far outnumbered Magellan's forces.

A fierce fight took place on the shore. Pigafetta, who was wounded in the forehead, described the scene: "They shot so many arrows at us and hurled so many bamboo spears (some tipped with iron) at the captain-general, besides fire-hardened, pointed stakes, stones and dirt, that we could scarcely defend ourselves. Seeing that, the captain-general sent some men to burn their houses in order to terrify them. When they saw their houses burning, they were roused to greater fury. . . . So many of them charged down upon us that they shot the captain through the right leg with a poisoned arrow."

Magellan fell. As he did, he ordered his army to retreat, but several loyal men stayed with their leader, whereupon seven were killed, including the boy who was probably Magellan's son, Cristovão Rebêlo. Lapulapu's men set upon the fallen captain-general, attacking him with spears and bolos, as he lay face downward on the shore, the waves of the sea washing over him. And that is how Ferdinand Magellan, the courageous explorer and great navigator, died.

Four centuries later Charles McKew Parr, a historian, wrote, "It was finished. The earthly destiny of Ferdinand Magellan had led him to voyage around the whole world to his death, and his last weeks of religious exaltation seem to have been almost premonitory. It was as if the reward of earthly riches he had striven for so hard and long was not worth the having to him; once it was in his

Death of Magellan. NORTH WIND PICTURE ARCHIVES

grasp his whole being turned away from it, toward the realms of the spirit."

Pigafetta lamented in his journal, "They killed our mirror, our light, our comfort, and our true guide." Many others grieved as well, including Humabon, who was reported to have wept.

Upon Magellan's death, according to his will, Enrique, who had suffered a minor wound, was now a free man. But he was so distraught at losing his master that he could neither eat nor work. To make matters worse, Duarte Barbosa, Magellan's brother-in-law and the *Trinidad*'s new captain, refused to recognize his freedom from bondage and forced him to work by threat of severe punishment. Enrique was so hurt and angered that he decided to take part in a vengeful plot.

After the Mactan massacre, Humabon realized that the Muslim merchant who had earlier warned him about the visitors had indeed offered wise advice. The Europeans had turned out to be more troublesome than they were worth, and Humabon decided it was time to get rid of them. Promising gifts of precious jewels, he invited the remaining officers to a banquet four days after Magellan's death. Two of them became suspicious early in the evening and escaped. They were the pilot Joâo Lopes Carvalho, who had once lived in Brazil, and Gonzalo Gómez de Espinosa, fleet master-at-arms and a steadfast follower of Magellan. The other officers, including Duarte Barbosa and João Serrão, were seized and murdered, reportedly by having their throats slit.

Now few officers and navigators were left. It seemed that the small fleet would never find its way home.

CHAPTER NINE
Hail, Victoria

With Magellan gone, the men's spirits sank to the lowest depths. Without their "light and true guide," what would become of them now?

After the banquet slaughter, they had no choice but to depart at once. They found, however, that the *Concepción* was so rotted from tropical water worms that she was beyond repair. But there were not enough crew to sail three ships anyway, so after unloading supplies, gear, and cargo they abandoned the vessel and set her afire. This delayed their departure two days.

Two ships were left—the *Trinidad* and the *Victoria*. Of the 270 men who had sailed from Spain at the start, only 107 remained. The pilot Joâo Lopes Carvalho was elected commander of the severely reduced fleet, while Gonzalo Gómez de Espinosa took command of the *Victoria*.

Without Magellan's seafaring abilities, the two well-worn ships sailed aimlessly from island to island, with the men collecting what food they could. But they never found enough to stave off constant hunger. Since they were sailing in Portuguese territory, they were always in fear of being caught by Portuguese sailors.

Desperate, they turned to piracy, capturing Chinese junks and Arab merchant ships, stealing food, looting gold, and abducting crew, whom the Europeans badly needed to help them sail. They also forced several women passengers aboard. The new captain-general, Lopes Carvalho, proved lacking in leadership, and he failed to win the respect of any of the men. When he began mistreating the captured women, the men agreed that they had had enough of him. Banding together, they rose up against him, removed him from command, and replaced him with Gómez de Espinosa. Espinosa managed to restore some discipline, although for months they continued to wander, stealing and looting as much as any pirates on the high seas.

Finally, they abducted a Malayan man, who claimed to know the location of the Spice Islands, and his little boy. They also seized two other men from a small island and forced them to act as pilots. Then the two ships headed through the Celebes Sea and into the Molucca Sea. A current carried them toward a small island. As they neared it, one of the pilots and the Malayan man and his son jumped overboard and began swimming toward shore. The little boy, however, slipped off his father's back and drowned. The men managed to escape.

One captive pilot remained. Under his guidance, the two ships continued their search until at last the mountains of the Moluccas—Ternate, Tidore, Mare, Moti, Makian—were sighted. The date was November 6, 1521. This was two years and two months after the fleet's departure from Spain. Albo recorded their position, and although it was impossible to be precise in determining longitude, his logbook remains an important historical document for following the tracks of the voyage. His logbook was the first proof showing that anyone had sailed that far west.

When the *Trinidad* and *Victoria* entered the harbor at Tidore before dawn two days later, they were greeted by the sultan, or local ruler, who declared his desire "always to be true friends." Pigafetta wrote, "We gave thanks to God and for our greeting we discharged all our artillery. It is no wonder that we should be so joyful after suffering travail and perils for so long." The mariners successfully traded, happily loading their two vessels with spices—the prize of their quest. The sultan would later permit several of the Europeans to remain and set up a trading post, called a *feitoria*.

Feitorias were not only trading posts but European establishments built like fortresses to serve also as military and commerce centers.

All this time the men had not forgotten Francisco Serrão, friend of Magellan from the war campaign years, who had settled on the island of Ternate in wealth and splendor. They were anxious to meet with him as soon as possible. But, alas, they learned that he had died only months earlier. He had been poisoned by Ternate's rival on Tidore, the sultan with whom they had just traded.

Hail, Victoria

During the island visits, chronicler Pigafetta continued recording his observations, noting that "the Moors have lived in Molucca for about fifty years, and before that heathens lived there, who had not put a value and price on the cloves." He also listed an abundance of foods found there: "Ginger, sago [their bread, which was made from tropical palm wood that they dried and granulated], rice,

---

Always the observer of culture, Pigafetta recorded many words of the Moorish people of Tidore. Some of them are:

lac — man	*adlo* — sun	*deghex* — honey
parampuam — woman	*songhot* — moon	*balus* — glass beads
guai — face	*mene* — dawn	*uzza* — one
matta — eyes	*taghai* — evening	*dua* — two
ilon — nose	*tau* — river	*tolo* — three
claio — fire	*coloncolon* — bell	*upat* — four
assu — smoke	*macan* — to eat	*lima* — five
tubin — water	*minuncubil* — to drink	*onom* — six
sanipan — boat	*monot* — chicken	*pitto* — seven
benaoa — ship	*candia* — goat	*guala* — eight
boloan — gold	*malissa* — pepper	*ciam* — nine
pilla — silver	*chiande* — cloves	*polo* — ten
mutiara — pearl	*mana* — cinnamon	
tatamue — wood	*tubu* — sugarcane	

---

goats, geese, poultry, coconuts, figs, almonds, larger than ours, sweet pomegranates, oranges, lemons, honey from bees as small as ants, who make their honey in trees—sugar cane, coconut oil, melons, cucumbers, sugar, a refreshing fruit as large as a gourd called a *comulicai* [mango]."

The men regained their health and strength quickly. And they were jubilant at finding the valuable spices that would bring them the profits they had dreamed of for so long. Finally, the ships were packed with all the cargo they could hold, and the men prepared to sail for home. But at departure, a seam in the *Trinidad* suddenly split wide open, and water rushed into the bilge. There was no time to make repairs. It was December. Monsoon storms were coming. The *Victoria* would have to sail alone.

The *Trinidad* remained with her crew in the Moluccas. (During that time Lopes Carvalho took ill and died.) When the ship was finally repaired, she set sail for Spain with fifty-four men under the command of Gonzalo Gómez de Espinosa. He reestablished order, but since he was unfamiliar with the winds and currents of the Sulu and Celebes Seas, he led the men blindly around and around for four months. They endured rough seas and punishing storms, hunger, and eventually death from exposure, exhaustion, and scurvy—one after another, until only twenty-one seamen were left.

Finally, they made their way back to the Moluccas. But danger from another source met them this time. Portuguese sailors seized the *Trinidad*, along with its enormous cargo of spices, and stripped her of her papers, charts, equipment, and light artillery. The remaining crew was imprisoned and left with nothing but the tattered clothing on their backs. Most of them were put to labor in *feitorias*. A few men disappeared. Four, including Gómez de Espinosa, made their way back to Spain some years later. Under the Portuguese, the *Trinidad* lived through one last storm. But when her anchor cable broke apart, she ended up running aground; her timbers were dismantled and used to reinforce the Portuguese fort built on Ternate.

Meanwhile the *Victoria*, loaded with spices, had departed the Moluccas the week of Christmas 1521. Her new captain was none other than Juan Sebastián del Cano, one of the mutineers who had risen up against Magellan at San Julián but whose life had been spared. The ship's crew numbered forty-seven Europeans and twelve islanders, with Moluccan pilots guiding her. The chronicler Pigafetta was also aboard.

But the *Victoria*, too, was struck by violent storms and suffered considerable damage. After two weeks she found anchorage on the island of Ombai (now called Alor), where the crew made repairs and traded with islanders for fresh food. From there they crossed the channel to Timor, needing to gather large stores of food for the upcoming voyage west across the Indian Ocean. Timor's chieftain set high prices for his livestock, though, and this angered the Spaniards so much that they seized him and held him for ransom until they had secured several pigs and goats. During the stay there two European sailors jumped ship rather than face another ocean journey.

Statue of Juan Sebastián del Cano. NORTH WIND PICTURE ARCHIVES

By now the new year, 1522, had arrived. In February the *Victoria* reached the Indian Ocean, where the seamen struggled day and night against cold and hunger. Thankfully, in May they sighted the African mainland. By then another four men had died. Hunger and exposure continued to plague the crew, and by the time the ship rounded the Cape of Good Hope, several more had perished.

Hail, Victoria

It was July when the *Victoria* approached the Cape Verde Islands, which was Portuguese territory. Elcano and his crew were desperate and had no choice but to anchor and send the longboat ashore for food. Thirteen men ventured forth, but they were caught and arrested as intruders. When they failed to return, Elcano had to sail on without them.

The crew was small, overworked, severely short of provisions, and sailing a crippled ship in ever-changing winds. And the death toll continued to rise. Yet they managed to stay afloat and remain on course for Spain.

At last, on September 6, 1522, the *Victoria,* the only ship to complete the voyage, entered the harbor at Sanlúcar de Barrameda. It had been almost three years to the day since she had departed with the other four ships of the fleet. She had journeyed 40,777 miles. Now she had come home.

Pigafetta wrote, "On Saturday the sixth of September, one thousand five hundred and twenty-two, we entered the Bay of San Lúcar, and we were only eighteen men [Europeans], the most part sick. From the time when we departed from Molucca until the present day we had sailed fourteen thousand four hundred and sixty leagues, and completed the circuit of the world from east to west."

The exact date of arrival created a mystery, however. The voyagers recorded it as September 6. But once they were in Spain, the calendar indicated that it was September 7. The mariners had been exact in their date-keeping, so this was truly puzzling and especially worrisome to them. For if they were a day off, had all their

The Victoria *was the first ship to circumnavigate the earth.*
THE MARINERS' MUSEUM, NEWPORT NEWS, VIRGINIA

religious observances and prayers been offered to the saints on the wrong days?

What accounted for the difference? After a few weeks of studies made independently by astronomers, court officials, and the chronicler Pigafetta, it was figured out that circumnavigating the globe meant either the loss or gain of a complete twenty-four-hour day.

This is because as a ship sails eastward, the sun rises four minutes *earlier* with each degree of longitude. Conversely, as a ship sails west, the sun rises four minutes *later* with each degree of longitude. Three hundred sixty degrees of longitude thus totals a twenty-four-hour period. The westward fleet had lost a full day.

The arrival of the *Victoria* in Spain was a momentous occasion. The joy and relief of the few remaining survivors (just twenty-one, including three Moluccans) was overwhelming. Immediately, the feeble, disheveled men were delivered food and wine, and a crew was employed to tow the battered ship up the Guadalquivir River to Seville.

Two days later, in Seville, the *Victoria* fired a final salute, and port authorities sent an armed guard to safeguard the ship and its precious cargo of spices. The following day the survivors who were able to walk marched in procession in shirts and bare feet, each man carrying a lighted torch, to shrines at the churches of Santa María de la Victoria and Santa María de Antigua. Before their departure the men had knelt solemnly in prayer, and now, after their long ordeal at sea, they offered thanks for their miraculous return.

The *Victoria* was the first ship ever to circumnavigate the earth. It was a cruel and bitter irony that the seafarer who completed this historical voyage had been Magellan's mutinous enemy, Elcano, and not Ferdinand Magellan himself.

CHAPTER TEN

After the Voyage

The Magellan story did not end with the explorer's death and the return of the *Victoria*. There were still more tales to tell. What happened to the ship and the survivors? What became of the members of the royal court? What befell Magellan's heirs?

The *Victoria*'s cargo of fifty-seven tons of spices, mostly cloves, paid for expenses of the entire journey—and earned a tidy profit as well, all of which the Crown claimed. Cristóbal de Haro acted as the Crown's business agent in selling the spices. He then spent eighteen years recovering the money that he had originally invested. The *Victoria* was patched up and made two more voyages, both to Santo Domingo, now the Dominican Republic, on the island of Hispaniola. Upon her last return she went down in a storm with all hands on board, never to be seen again.

Juan Sebastián del Cano, Elcano, was summoned to court in Valladolid and appeared along with the pilot, Francisco Albo, and Hernando de Bustamante, a barber who had also served as medic and surgeon. All received honors, but Elcano was hailed as a hero and presented with a coat of arms and offered an annual pension. Later Elcano returned to sea as a pilot and tried to follow Magellan's tracks to the Moluccas. Even though he knew what to expect this time, miseries abounded on that voyage, too, including a siege of scurvy. In the summer of 1526 his scurvy-ravaged body was buried at sea in the Pacific Ocean.

The crewmen who had been arrested by the Portuguese on the Cape Verde Islands were rescued by a squadron that King Charles dispatched. Neither they nor the other survivors received any pay beyond their scheduled wages. The families of the seamen who had died were given no compensation, either.

Gonzalo Gómez de Espinosa, the loyal seaman who had helped Magellan during the San Julián mutiny and commanded the *Trinidad* after Magellan's death, was one of the crew captured by Portuguese in the Moluccas. He was put to hard labor in one *feitoria* after another for four years. He was released, he returned to Spain, where he was promised a pension, but he was not paid until years later. It was reported that he lived out his life in comfort in the parish of San Nicolás in Seville.

Elcano's signature is found on his will, signed and sealed at sea on July 26, 1526. He died of scurvy only days later. The other signatures belong to witnesses.

———

Magellan and Beatriz's first child, Rodrigo, died in 1521 while Magellan was at sea. Their second child was stillborn. Beatriz herself died soon after learning of her husband's death; she never knew of the *Victoria*'s return. No record exists of Magellan's brother or sister having made claims to their rightful inheritance. Neither of them had children. Magellan's father-in-law, Diogo Barbosa, who had invested in the enterprise shortly before the fleet's departure, was unable to claim any compensation for himself.

The fate of Enrique, Magellan's faithful slave, is unknown.

Bishop Juan Rodríguez de Fonseca continued in his corrupt and misbegotten ways at court. After changing official documents and forging signatures once too often, he was finally dismissed from office by the pope. He passed the rest of his life secluded in study.

King Manuel I of Portugal died of a fever in 1521, the same year Magellan died. He was succeeded by his son, John (João) III.

Charles I, King of Spain/Charles V, Emperor of the Holy Roman Empire, married Isabella, the sister of the new Portuguese ruler, John III, in 1526. This brought to a close the bitter rivalry between the two nations. Charles died in 1558.

According to the Treaty of Tordesillas, the Moluccas were located in the "Portuguese hemisphere." For a while Spain insisted on claiming the Spice Islands, but ultimately there was no way to take possession of the islands or to establish an empire there. In 1529, because of an impoverished Spanish crown that had been drained by war campaigns, King Charles ceded all claims to the islands to Portugal for 350,000 gold ducats. The arrangement was signed in secrecy, which angered businessmen Haro and Fugger because they continued in commercial trading. Portugal ruled the spice trade of the Moluccas until the middle of the seventeeth century, when the Dutch East India Company forcibly seized control.

Antonio Pigafetta assembled his journal writings into a manuscript he titled *The First Voyage Around the World* and sought patronage for its publication. He was not invited to the Spanish court but made the journey on his own. When Charles agreed to see him, Pigafetta said that he had something "not gold or silver, but things more precious in the eyes of so great a sovereign." Then he offered "a book written by my hand, concerning all the matters that had occurred from day to day during our voyage." Afterward, Pigafetta traveled to Portugal, presenting a copy of his book to the new king, João III; to France, where he gave a copy to Louise of Savoy, mother of the king, Francois I; and finally, to his own nation of Italy, where he worked on yet another version at his home in Vicenza. In 1524, Pope Clement VII summoneded Pigafetta to Rome to hear the story for himself.

Although three courts accepted Pigafetta's gift, none granted him patronage or arranged for the printing of his journal during his lifetime. The original copy, written in Spanish and Italian, has not survived. Three French copies and one Italian copy still exist.

The journal contains 104 entries, noting Pigafetta's observations, encounters, and viewpoints, as well as twenty-three illustrations, mostly of islands in the East Indies. Each illustration is linked with a written passage. *The First Voyage Around the World* has been described as a "marvel-filled unity of travel narrative and geographical account."

Many stories are told of Pigafetta's life after his visit to Rome, but his fate remains unknown.

Francisco Albo's log, *Diary or Pilot's Log Book of the Voyage of Ferdinand Magellan*, is a straightforward report of navigational sight readings and determinations of positions. It is one of the most significant documents of the voyage. Albo's first entry is dated November 29, 1519: "I began to take the altitude of sun whilst following the said voyage; and whilst in the vicinity of Cape St. Augustine." He concluded on September 4, 1522, when they sighted the Cape Verde Islands in the North Atlantic Ocean. Albo made only one copy of his diary. Following his court appearance, he returned to his birthplace of Axio on the Greek Island of Rhodes. He may have entered into Turkish service.

Another log was kept between Spain and the Moluccas, but it was confiscated by the Portuguese. The original has disappeared; however, three copies have survived. It was written by a Genoese pilot, but there is no proof of authorship.

———

Other accounts of the circumnavigation exist, but they were written by historians of the time and not by crew or eyewitnesses. Maximilian of Transylvania was a secretary in the Spanish court when the *Victoria* returned, and he may have helped prepare the reception for Elcano; he wrote a brief version of the voyage, as he had heard it told, in a letter to his father. The letter was written in Latin and dated October 22, 1522. Portuguese historians Gaspar Correa and João de Barros wrote narratives using documents that the Portuguese had seized on the *Trinidad*. Peter Martyr (Pietro Martire d'Anghiera), an Italian who had lived at the Spanish court in the service of King Ferdinand and Queen Isabella, and who was also a tutor of Maximilian of Transylvania, compiled Spanish sea stories. His story of Magellan's journey was sent to Rome to be printed, but it was destroyed during the sacking of Rome in 1527 by invading imperial troops of Emperor Charles V.

Ferdinand Magellan, the great explorer, was neither recognized nor paid honor until long after his death. His devoted friends who had survived, including Pigafetta, were too few in number and too weak in influence to enable the account of his accomplishments to rise above the criticism.

Certainly the expedition had brought great suffering and ruin, but in Spain many of the sailors who had deserted the fleet with the *San Antonio* spread lies and exaggerated stories about Magellan that darkened his legacy for years. In Portugal King Manuel denounced

Coat of arms and signature of Magellan. NORTH WIND PICTURE ARCHIVES

Map showing new understanding of the world's dimensions, created by Battista Agnese in Venice, about 1544. Magellan's voyage, which is traced in black, is commemorated under the guidance of the twelve winds of antiquity.

Magellan until his last breath, making sure that his countrymen would long consider the explorer a traitor.

As time passed, though, and people began to reconcile old, preconceived ideas with new views of the world, they started to grasp the magnitude of Magellan's achievement and contributions. In sailing west to the Spice Islands, he proved empirically that the world is not only round but circumnavigable. He added to navigational and geographical knowledge. He found the seaway passage later named the Strait of Magellan and observed the Magellanic Clouds that bear his name. Finally, he became universally recognized as a master navigator and scientific explorer. Now he is honored for his courage and daring. Above all, his story is acclaimed as a triumph of the human spirit.

Ferdinand Magellan was a "valiant and noble captain," wrote Pigafetta. "No other had so much natural boldness or knowledge to sail once around the world."

FERNANDO DE MAGALLANES.

Magellan. THE MARINERS' MUSEUM, NEWPORT NEWS, VIRGINIA

CHRONOLOGY OF EVENTS

1480(?)   Birth of Ferdinand Magellan in northern Portugal
            (exact year is unknown)

1488   Bartolomeu Dias, Portuguese navigator, sails around the
            Cape of Good Hope, the southern tip of Africa

1492   Christopher Columbus, Italian explorer who sailed under the
            Spanish flag, sets out on the first of four voyages westward,
            making historic landfall on an island in the Bahamas

            Magellan enters into service as a page in the royal court of
            Portugal

1493   Pope Alexander VI divides the unexplored world between
            Portugal and Spain in a papal line of demarcation; a year later,
            in the Treaty of Tordesillas, the line moved 1,000 leagues west

1497–99   Vasco da Gama, Portuguese mariner, reaches India, opening
            direct sea route to the East Indies

1505–13   Magellan sails with Portuguese war fleet to Africa and India

1513   Vasco Nuñez de Balboa, Spanish explorer, crosses the Isthmus
            of Panama and sights the Great South Sea (Pacific Ocean)

1517   Magellan leaves Portugal for Spain, seeking support for his enterprise to sail west to the Spice Islands (Moluccas)

1518   King Charles I of Spain agrees to finance Magellan's expedition and provides a fleet of five ships

Magellan marries Beatriz Barbosa

1519   Magellan, captain-general of the fleet, sets out to discover a new sea route to the Spice Islands

Fleet crosses the equator into the southern hemisphere

1520   Magellan sails through the strait (near the tip of South America) that is named for him and enters the Great South Sea, which he renames the Pacific Ocean

1521   Magellan is killed April 27 on the Philippine Island of Mactan

1522   The *Victoria*, the only surviving ship of the fleet, completes the first circumnavigation of the earth

BIBLIOGRAPHY

Albo, Francisco. "Extracts from a *Derrotero* or Log-Book of the Voyage of Fernando de Magallanes in Search of the Strait, from the Cape of St. Augustin." In *The First Voyage Round the World by Magellan*. London: Hakluyt Society, 1874.

Boorstin, Daniel J. *The Discoverers: A History of Man's Search to Know His World and Himself*. New York: Random House, 1983.

Guillemard, F. H. H. *The Life of Ferdinand Magellan and the First Circumnavigation of the Globe: 1480–1521*. London, 1890 (Reprint: New York: AMS Press, 1971).

Hermann, Paul. *The Great Age of Discovery*. Translated by Arnold Jo Pomerans. New York: Harper & Row, 1958.

Joyner, Tim. *Magellan*. Camden, Me.: International Marine Publishing, 1992.

Kemp, Peter. *The History of Ships*. London: Orbis Publishing Ltd., 1978 (Reprint: New York: Galahad Books, 1979).

Levinson, Nancy Smiler. *Christopher Columbus: Voyager to the Unknown*. New York: Lodestar, 1990.

BIBLIOGRAPHY

Morison, Samuel Eliot. *The Great Explorers: The European Discovery of America: The Southern Voyages 1492–1616.* New York: Oxford, 1974.

Nowell, Charles E., ed. *Magellan's Voyage Around the World: Three Contemporary Accounts.* Evanston, Ill.: Northwestern University Press, 1962.

———. *Portugal.* Englewood Cliffs, N.J.: Prentice-Hall, 1973.

Parker, John. *Discovery: Developing Views of the Earth from Ancient Times to the Voyages of Captain Cook.* New York: Charles Scribner's Sons, 1972.

Parr, Charles McKew. *So Noble a Captain: The Life and Times of Ferdinand Magellan.* New York: Crowell, 1953.

Pérez-Mallaína, Pablo E. *Spain's Men of the Sea: Daily Life on the Indies Fleets in the Sixteenth Century.* Translated by Carla Rahn Phillips. Baltimore: Johns Hopkins, 1998.

Pigafetta, Antonio. *The First Voyage Around the World (1519–1522): An Account of Magellan's Expedition.* Theodore J. Cachey Jr., ed. New York: Marsilio, 1995.

———. *Magellan's Voyage: A Narrative of the First Circumnavigation.* Translated and edited by R. A. Skelton. New York: Dover, 1994.

Silverberg, Robert. *The Longest Voyage: Circumnavigators in the Age of Discovery.* Indianapolis and New York: Bobbs-Merrill, 1972.

Stefoff, Rebecca. *Ferdinand Magellan and the Discovery of the World Ocean.* New York: Chelsea House, 1990.

Wilford, John Noble. *The Mapmakers.* New York: Knopf, 1981 (Reprint: New York: Random House, 1982).

SOURCE NOTES

Historians and researchers of a sea voyage that took place five centuries ago cannot expect to find many primary sources or first-hand accounts. There are only a few, and the journals and correspondence, written in several languages, differ greatly. Much of a recounted story depends on secondhand reports, incomplete records, and conjecture based on what is understood about the background and customs of the time.

While few records of Magellan's early life exist, many documents pertaining to the expedition are available. Most of them are catalogued in the Archivo General de Indias in Seville, Spain. Charles McKew Parr in *So Noble a Captain: The Life and Times of Ferdinand Magellan*, pages 398–401, lists sixty-seven sources that are the most pertinent to Magellan's voyage. Included are letters and letter fragments, royal orders, accounts of payment, receipts for funds or supplies, and documentation of spices brought back on the *Victoria*.

Also catalogued are numerous court records of litigation filed against the Spanish Crown after the expedition by survivors, heirs, and investors claiming due wages or compensation for their investment in the undertaking. Parr points out that these court records shed important additional light on the expedition.

Source Notes

General

The Warwick Atlas of World History, Jane Olliver, ed. (New York: Warwick Press, 1988), includes concise maps, drawings, photographs, and time charts from travel and trade in Europe and Asia to the discovery of the New World.

Online resources about the Age of Exploration can be found at *http://voyager.snc.edu/voyager2/explore.html.*

Chapter 1: Young Man of Portugal

Balboa's full story is told by Jeannette Mirsky in *The Westward Crossings* (New York: Knopf, 1946), Part I, "Gold for the Crown," pages 7–108.

Prince Henry 'the Navigator': A Life by Peter Russell (New Haven and London: Yale University Press, 2000) is an extensive, scholarly work. The author was director of Portuguese Studies at the University of Oxford and is a Commander of the Order of Prince Henry.

For one explanation of the beginning of Portuguese slave trade in Africa, John Parker notes in *Discovery: Developing Views of the Earth from Ancient Times to the Voyages of Captain Cook* that as a result of Prince Henry's need to learn more about Africa and its trade routes from natives, in 1441 he ordered that Africans be captured and brought to Portugal. See chapter 10, "Prince Henry the Navigator."

Chapter 2: War Campaigns at Sea

The Columbia History of the World, John A. Garraty and Peter Gay, eds. (New York: Harper & Row, 1972), offers a broad look at the period of competition of commercial powers, especially regarding Portugal.

CHAPTER 3: THE GREAT ENTERPRISE

A good interactive source on early navigation methods and navigation instruments is the Web site of the Mariners' Museum, Newport News, Virginia: *www.mariner.org/age/earlynav.html*.

A story about John Harrison and his work is found in Dava Sobel's *Longtitude: The Story of a Lone Genius Who Solved the Greatest Scientific Problem of His Time* (New York: Walker, 1995).

CHAPTER 4: FITTING OUT THE FLEET

Extensive lists of stores and equipment of the fleet can be found in the appendixes in F. H. H. Guillemard's book, *The Life of Ferdinand Magellan and the First Circumnavigation of the Globe: 1480–1521*, pages 329–36.

Although the number of crew that departed is not conclusive, a roster of 241 names is included in Tim Joyner's *Magellan*, Appendix 3A, pages 252–63. He adds that some men were recruited in the Canary Islands.

CHAPTER 5: THE VOYAGE BEGINS

Jean-Paul Duvoils's essay "The Patagonian 'Giants'" summarizes the various myths about the people of Patagonia in *Patagonia, Natural History, Prehistory and Ethnography at the Uttermost End of the Earth*, Colin McEwan, Luis A Borrero, and Alfredo Prieto, eds. (Princeton: Princeton University Press, 1997), pages 127–39.

An old Spanish chivalric tale of an island giant called Patagón is the basis for another explanation of the origin of the name "Patagons," cited by Maria Rosa de Malkiel in "Para la Toponimía argentina; Patagonia," *Hispanic Review*, XX, 1952.

CHAPTER 6: DESTINED FOR DANGER

Charles Darwin's quotation is from *The Voyage of the Beagle* (New York: New American Library, Inc., 1972), page 199. In the account of his journey, he includes an entire chapter describing the strait: "Strait of Magellan, Climate of the Southern Coasts."

CHAPTER 7: THE ENDLESS OCEAN

It is interesting to read the first-person account of James Lind's studies that led to his discovery of the cause of scurvy. *A Treatise of the Scurvy, 1753* by the Scottish naval physician can be found on the Internet at *http://pc-78-120.udac.se:8001/www/Nautica/Medicine/Lind(1753).html*.

CHAPTER 8: TRAGIC DEATH

The island of Tandaya was called Filipinas by the conquistador Ruy Lopez de Villalobos in 1543 for his future king, Felipe (Phillip) II of Spain, according to the *Historical Dictionary of the Philippines*, by Artemio Guillermo and May Kyi Win (Lanham, Maryland, and London: The Scarecrow Press, Inc., 1997), page 191.

Pigafetta's journal puts the number of men killed in battle, in addition to Magellan, at eight. In *Magellan's Voyage: A Narrative of the First Circumnavigation*, page 164, R. A. Skelton notes that one historian names seven men and adds one who died later of wounds.

CHAPTER 9: HAIL, VICTORIA

In *The Life of Ferdinand Magellan and the First Circumnavigation of the Globe: 1480–1521*, page 281, F. H. H. Guillemard suggests two other possible causes of Francisco Serrão's death: he was poisoned by a Malayan woman acting under Portuguese orders or, because he was becoming too powerful, he was sent back to India and died on board ship.

Chapter 10: After the Voyage

In *Magellan's Voyage Around the World: Three Contemporary Accounts*, Charles Nowell remarks, page 331, that Elcano's first thought upon landing was to send a report to the emperor, Charles V, to give his account of the voyage. Apparently, he hoped to assure himself of recognition. He also asked that the survivors be allowed to keep their profits from the spices brought into port, without having to pay the customary duties and royal share of profits.

Regarding Maximilian of Transylvania's letter, Nowell adds to the weight of its importance, noting, page 5, that it was the first information on the voyage made available to the people of Europe.

INDEX

Page numbers in **bold** type refer to illustrations.